W0082273

NEIL ZLOZOWER/ATLASICONS.COM

VAN HALEN

★ **40 YEARS OF THE GREAT AMERICAN ROCK BAND** ★

Copyright © 2012 Time Home Entertainment Inc.

Published by Time Home Entertainment Inc.
135 West 50th Street • New York, NY 10020

All rights reserved. No part of this book may be
reproduced in any form or by any electronic or
mechanical means, including information storage
and retrieval systems, without permission in
writing from the publisher, except by a reviewer,
who may quote brief passages in a review.

ISBN 10: 1-61893-027-3
ISBN 13: 978-1-61893-027-9

We welcome your comments and suggestions
about Time Home Entertainment Books.
Please write to us at:
Time Home Entertainment Books, Attention:
Book Editors, P.O. Box 11016, Des Moines, IA
50336-1016

If you would like to order any of our hardcover
Collector's Edition books, please call us at
1-800-327-6388, Monday through Friday, 7 a.m. to
8 p.m., or Saturday, 7 a.m. to 6 p.m., Central Time.

Cover design: Alexis Cook
Book design: Michael Wilson
Cover photography: Scott Weiner/Retna Ltd.

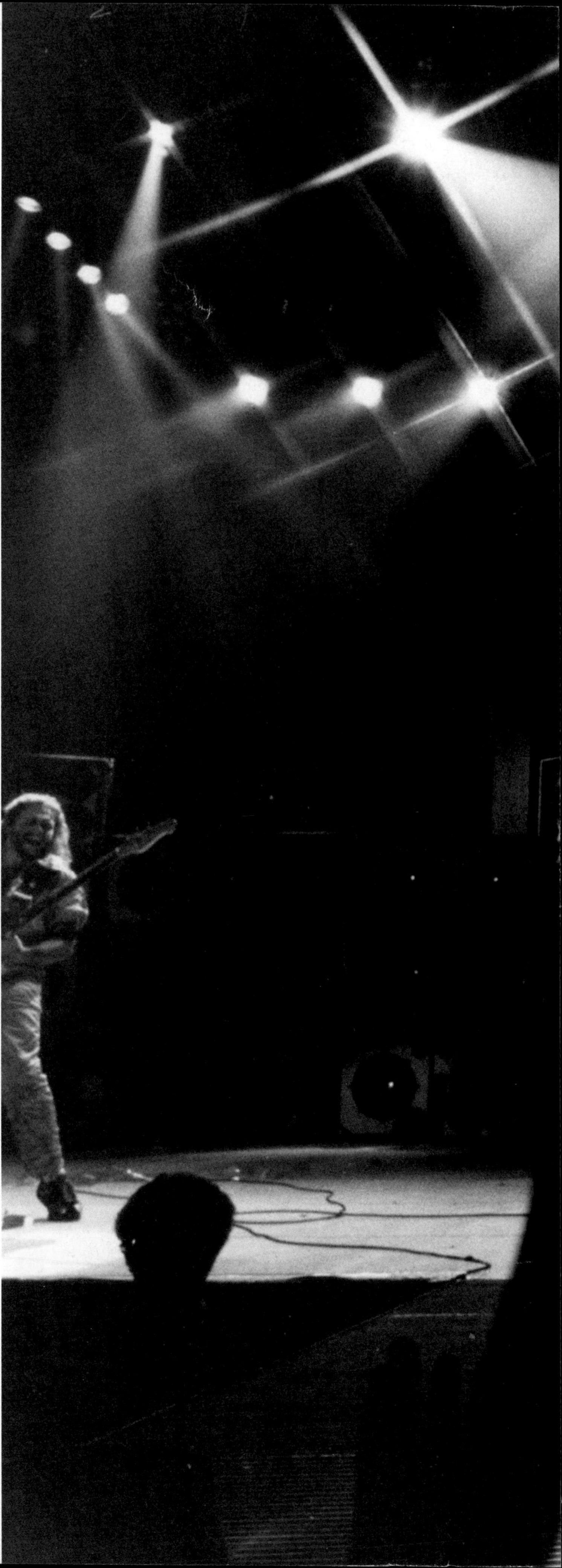

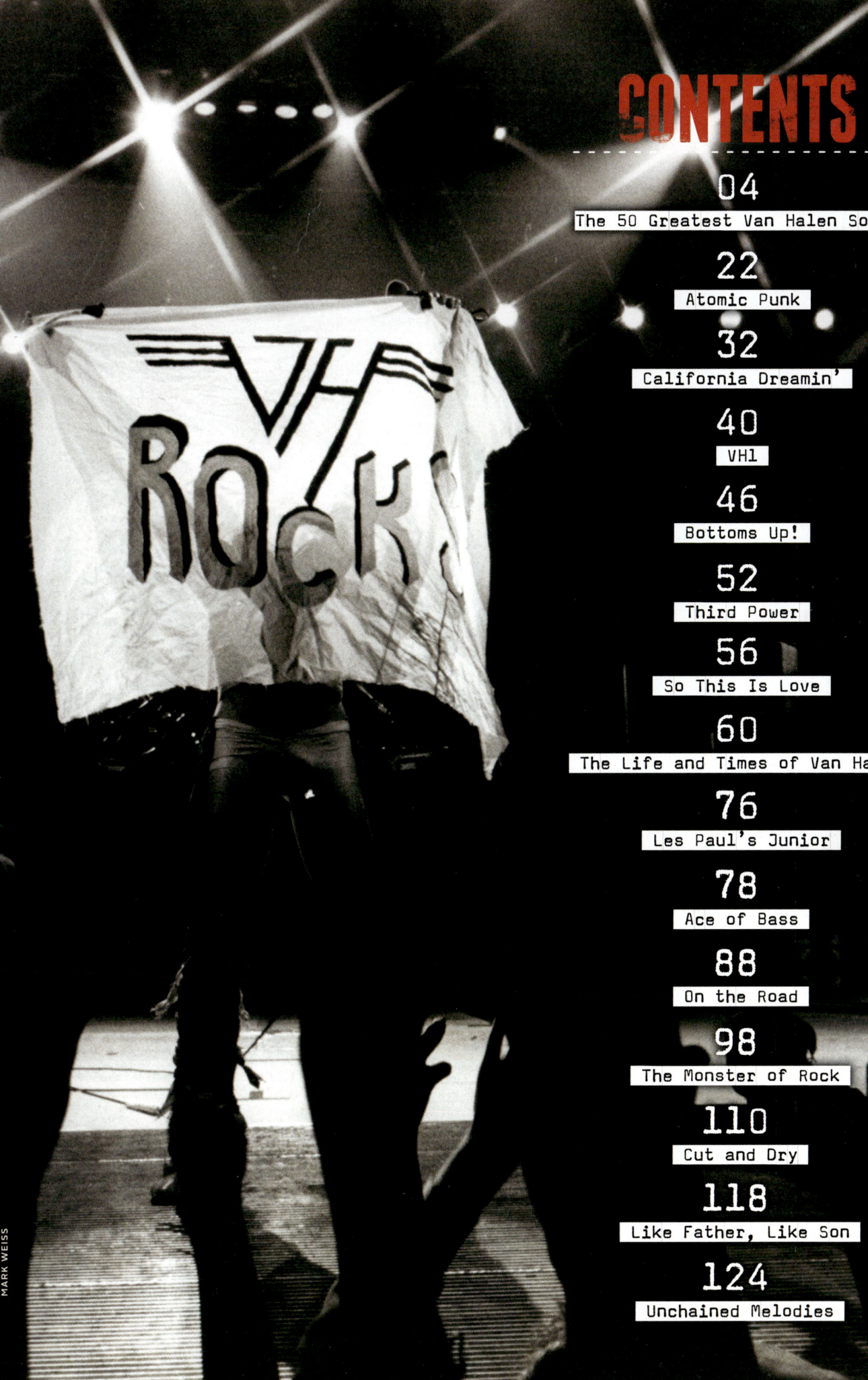

CONTENTS

MARK WEISS

THE 50 GREATEST VAN HALEN SONGS

Guitar World celebrates Van Halen's greatest tracks of all time, from "Runnin' with the Devil" to "Tattoo."

- - - - -

ROSS HALFIN

NEIL ZLOZOWER/ATLASICONS.COM

1

HOT FOR TEACHER

1984 1984

A **QUINTESSENTIAL** classic Van Halen song must have several crucial elements: thundering drums, rumbling bass that is felt more than heard, an outrageously cocky vocal performance, a killer guitar riff, and an acrobatic guitar solo with more thrills and spills than Evel Knievel jumping 25 explosive-filled cars with a dirt bike and a fifth of Jack Daniel's. "Hot for Teacher" delivers all of these elements in spades, making it the definitive Van Halen song (and making its omission from the 1996 *Best of Volume 1* collection a criminal oversight).

The song begins with a bang, with Alex Van Halen pummeling a rapid-fire double-kick intro that sounds more like a dragster warming up for a race than a drum kit. Eddie kicks the dynamics up a notch, furiously tapping his Flying V's fretboard before blasting off into power-chord overdrive. The song's real appeal, however, lies in its infectious nitro-fueled boogie-blues shuffle, which sounds like ZZ Top juiced on methamphetamines and Viagra. "That song was beyond any boogie I ever heard," Eddie recalls. "It was pretty powerful." David Lee Roth walks a tightrope between macho metal posturing and tongue-in-cheek humor, making a possibly obscene scenario seem absurd and even charming.

Eddie's solo is pure excitement, distinguished by dazzling ascending runs and a loose, flowing feel that makes even his most challenging passages sound effortless and unforced. The boisterous climax, lifted from the band's 1977 demo of "Voodoo Queen," is an aural orgasm that probably left most first-time listeners shouting "Oh my god!" in weak-kneed unison with Roth.

YNGWIE
MALMSTEEN
↓

"The first
Van Halen song
I heard was
'Ain't Talkin'
'Bout Love.'
I WENT,
'THAT RIFF
IS **GOOOOD**.'"

⟨ 2 AIN'T TALKIN' 'BOUT LOVE VAN HALEN 1978 ⟩

MUCH AS SLASH HAS GONE on record saying that his legendary guitar intro to "Sweet Child O' Mine" was written as a joke, Eddie Van Halen has downplayed "Ain't Talkin' 'Bout Love" as "just a stupid thing. Just two chords." But to paraphrase Spinal Tap, there's a fine line between stupid and clever. And this classic cut from Van Halen's 1978 debut (as well as Slash's work on "Sweet Child," for that matter) falls firmly into the latter category.

"Ain't Talkin' 'Bout Love" was one of the last songs written for *Van Halen*, and Eddie originally conceived the straightforward, two-chord basher (the majority of the song follows a basic Am-G chord progression) as a knock on the then-burgeoning punk

movement. But apparently "punk rock" as played by Eddie Van Halen includes an opening riff built on heavily palm-muted, arpeggiated chords, a third-verse breakdown filled with chiming harmonics, and a hooky, almost vocal-like guitar solo that, on the album version, Eddie doubled with a Coral electric sitar. Of playing the sitar, he recalls, "It sounded like a buzzy-fretted guitar. The thing was real bizarre."

In the end, perhaps the joke was on Ed, as "Love" has gone on to become one of Van Halen's most iconic tunes. In addition to being a classic-rock radio staple, it's been played on almost every tour the band has done with Roth. And in perhaps an even greater testament to its popularity, it was one of the few DLR-era songs that remained in live sets during the Sammy Hagar years.

NEIL ZLOZOWER/ATLASICONS.COM (VAN HALEN); TRAVIS SHINN (MALMSTEEN)

‹ 3 UNCHAINED FAIR WARNING 1981 ›

U NCHAINED" IS NOT JUST a welcome major-key party anthem in the middle of the moody *Fair Warning*—it's the Van Halen song that sold a million MXR M-117 stomp boxes. By carefully setting the flanger speed to sweep up in pitch on one half of the main riff and down on the next, Eddie created a rising-and-falling rollercoaster vibe that gave the fans a chance to throw their hands in the air and go along for the wild ride. A short, surprisingly restrained solo begins with some flash but quickly swings straight into melodic territory, bringing the break to a crisp crescendo. The song makes a perfect showcase for Roth's swagger, Michael Anthony's harmonies, Alex's percussive thunder, and, per Eddie's choice on this album, plenty of guitar over-dubs. And hearing Eddie play several guitar parts at once is just more of a good thing.

Whether the ad-libbed conversation between Dave and the apparently sharp-dressed producer Ted Templeman was really a spontaneous creation or a rehearsed bit is still up for discussion, but it hardly matters—it's proof that the band's playful personality was still in evidence, despite a widening rift between producer and artist. "I felt at the time that [*Templeman*] didn't understand me anymore," Eddie says. "I'd get so frustrated at not being able to do what I wanted. I ended up doing 90 percent of the guitar tracking at four o'clock in the morning with our engineer, Donn Landee." They say adversity inspires greatness, and with "Unchained," the ire clearly fueled the fire.

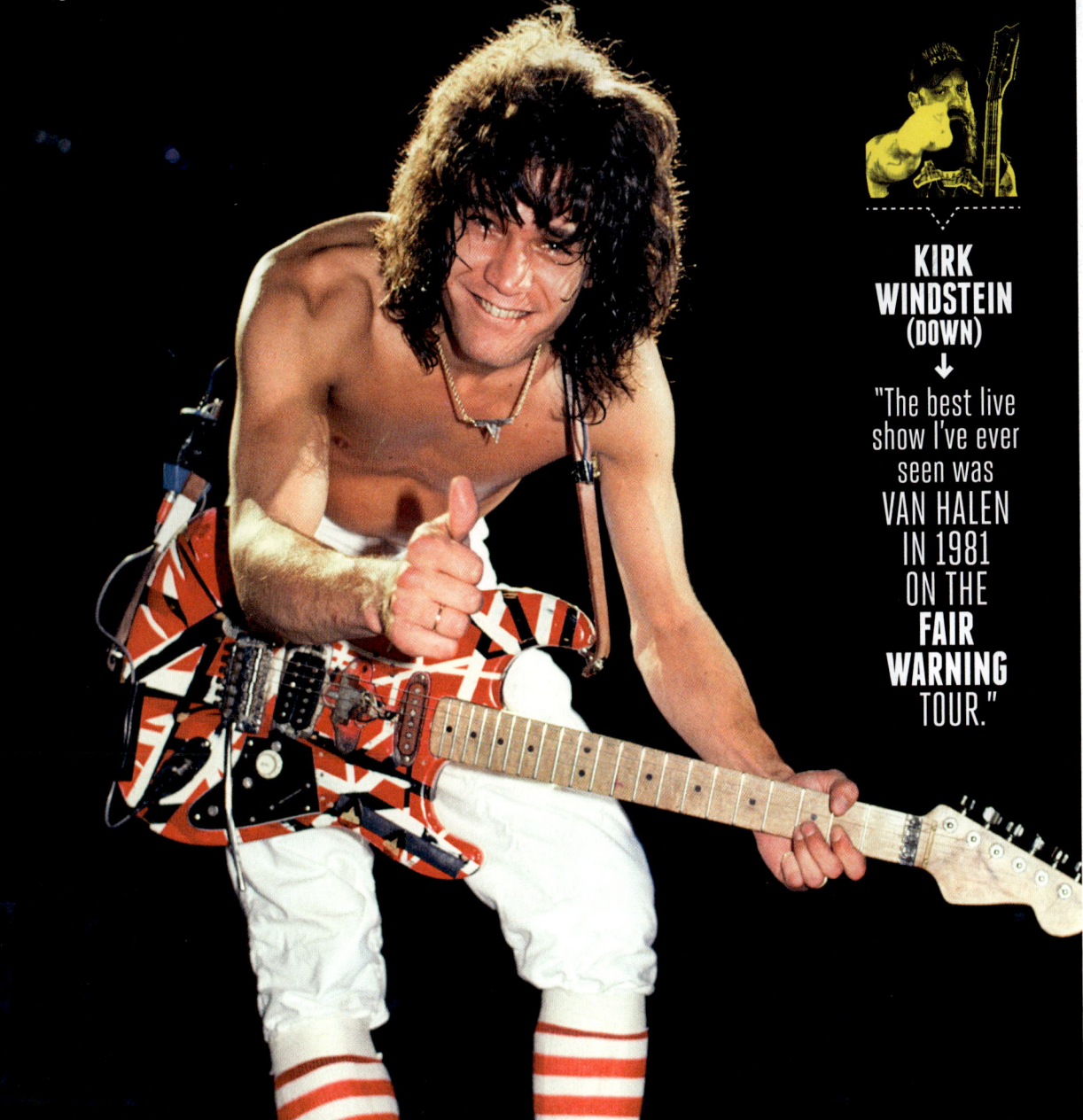

KIRK WINDSTEIN (DOWN)

↓

"The best live show I've ever seen was VAN HALEN IN 1981 ON THE FAIR WARNING TOUR."

NEIL ZLOZOWER/ATLASICONS.COM (VAN HALEN); JIMMY HUBBARD (WINDSTEIN)

4 BEAUTIFUL GIRLS VAN HALEN II 1979

BACK IN THE SEVENTIES and Eighties, most aspiring bands enjoyed the honorable rite of passage of playing at strip clubs and wet T-shirt contests. Alas, this privilege has now passed on to that instrument-deficient breed of plankton known as the DJ, but while it lasted it was one of the best gigs an up-and-coming musician could hope to get (especially if you managed to get lucky after the show).

"It was one of the reasons why we played," Alex recently explained. "It's just life. It's seeing everything, enjoying it, and taking it a little bit further than it should. You had to do the wet T-shirt contest during the fourth set. You had to get the girls lubed up, and then they would get looser and start to hike their skirts up."

Beyond good timing, it's important to know what songs will bring out a woman's inhibitions. While Van Halen had plenty of songs that could fill the bill, they went one better by writing their own ode to ogling called "Bring on the Girls" with a bump-and-grind riff, raunchy rhythm and lascivious lyrics guaranteed to get those sweater puppies shaking.

Due to record label pressure, the band toned down the lyrics slightly from the 1977 demo version and renamed the song "Beautiful Girls" when they recorded it for *Van Halen II*. But as anyone who has ever patronized the Seventh Veil or Spearmint Rhino can attest, the song still gets heavy rotation whenever some young lovely named Candy (or was that Cindy? Vicki?) takes the stage. And don't forget to tip your waitress.

NEIL ZLOZOWER/ATLASICONS.COM

FIN COSTELLO/REDFERNS/GETTY IMAGES (VAN HALEN); TRAVIS SHINN (MORTON)

‹ 5 RUNNIN' WITH THE DEVIL VAN HALEN ›

ON THE TWO OCCASIONS that Van Halen recorded this song as a demo—first with Gene Simmons producing in 1976 and again in 1977 with Ted Templeman and Mo Ostin as producers—it came directly after "House of Pain." The intro's unique dissonant, descending sound effect, created using a collection of car horns and tape manipulation, was actually the ending of "House of Pain," and the car horns appeared briefly throughout that song. While the effect was somewhat distracting between songs, Templeman realized it would make a brilliant attention-getting intro, so he decided to sequence "Runnin' with the Devil" as the first song on Van Halen's debut album.

With its basic chord progression and melodic guitar "solos,"

"Runnin' with the Devil" is one of the simplest songs Van Halen ever recorded, but like "Smoke on the Water" and "Iron Man," a big part of its power comes from that simplicity. Yet, to paraphrase Roth's lyrics, the simple things weren't so simple. Little embellishments—like the harmonized vocals on the chorus, the rhythm section's deep groove that swings as much as it stomps, and even the way Eddie rakes the strings between the bridge and stop tailpiece on his Ibanez Destroyer on the intro—make Van Halen's recording nearly inimitable. Perhaps the most striking feature of this song is Van Halen's raw, violent and hungry attitude. It's the kind of thing that only exists during that magical make-or-break moment when a band announces its presence to the world at large.

MARK MORTON → "The first couple of Van Halen records really set the bar for me. Eddie's work was the benchmark for a long time in terms of how far and how radically players were going to take soloing as an acrobatic exercise."

the first time a guitar player ever tapped, it is at least the first time people heard a guitarist tap for a good half minute. To this day, it's the yardstick by which all shred-fests are measured.

9

YOU REALLY GOT ME
VAN HALEN

VAN HALEN'S COVER of the Kinks' "You Really Got Me" premiered on L.A. radio station KMET months before their debut album. Allegedly, it was rush released because Eddie let Barry Brandt of Angel hear the track, which inspired Angel to record their own version. "It bummed me out that our first single was somebody else's tune," Ed says. Even so, Van Halen made the song their own with three-part harmony vocals, Ed's raucous guitar tone, and the first taste of his revolutionary tapping technique. No wonder Angel's version never materialized.

10

AND THE CRADLE WILL ROCK...
WOMEN AND CHILDREN FIRST
1980

THE HARD-ROCKING "Cradle" was actually Eddie's first foray into using keyboards on a Van Halen song. He performed the rhythm part on a Wurlitzer electric piano, fed into his MXR Flanger and cranked through his 100-watt Marshall. The resulting sound was oddly guitar-like and contributed to the song's haunting vibe. Still, Eddie received blowback from some of his bandmates. "They didn't want a 'guitar hero' playing keyboards," he recalled. "And that kind of ties in with why they didn't want 'Jump.'"

6

MEAN STREET
FAIR WARNING

ORIGINALLY RECORDED as a demo called "Voodoo Queen," "Mean Street" was reworked with darker lyrics, a dramatic chorus and a bridge lifted from early versions of "She's the Woman," the song the group unveiled during their performance at New York City's Cafe Wha? this past January. Ed's outrageous intro was inspired by funk slap bass. "I tapped on the 12th fret of the low E and the 12th fret of the high E and muffled both with my left hand down by the nut," he says.

7

PANAMA
1984

"PANAMA" IS Van Halen being quintessentially Van Halen. Roth is all brash swagger, with the hottest ride on the block. And, hey—he may have just stolen your girl, too! Musically, Eddie's riffing, paired with the propulsive rhythm, is the aural equivalent of burnin' down the avenue full blast with the top down. And that *whooshing* sound heard during Dave's midsong soliloquy? That would be the engine of Eddie's Lamborghini, with microphones on the exhaust pipes.

8

ERUPTION
VAN HALEN

THE FIRST FEW seconds are practically a direct lift from the intro to "Let Me Swim" by Seventies boogie rockers Cactus. But what follows is arguably the most inventive, groundbreaking and utterly mind-blowing rock guitar demonstration of the past 35 years. Eddie's instrumental *tour de force* explodes with lightning-fast runs, screaming pinch harmonics, insane dive bombs, nods to 18th-century violin etudes and furious tremolo picking, among other techniques. And if the song doesn't necessarily represent

JOHN 5 → "VAN HALEN OPENED UP SO MANY DOORS FOR ME.
Before that, I was mostly playing a lot of bluesy Hendrix-type stuff. But after hearing 'Eruption,' I turned into a total Van Halen nut, doing the whole Kramer-and-Floyd Rose thing. Van Halen changed the way I looked at the guitar, its sound—everything."

ED KRAMER/WIREIMAGE/GETTY IMAGES (VAN HALEN); ROBERT KNIGHT ARCHIVE/REDFERNS/GETTY IMAGES (JOHN 5)

11
LIGHT UP THE SKY
`VAN HALEN II`

BOTH EDDIE AND Alex proclaimed this their favorite *Van Halen II* track in 1979 due to what Eddie called its "progressive" feel. "The changes are a little more bent than the commercial stuff." True enough: the introductory stair-step joust between guitar and bass heralds wide dynamic shifts between quiet passages, balls-out rock riffage and a drum breakdown, capped by a solo full of tremolo picking and precise whammy waggles. There's a lot of drama in these three minutes.

12
EVERYBODY WANTS SOME!!
`WOMEN AND CHILDREN FIRST`

VAN HALEN AT their most primal. Alex pounds out a tribal beat, DLR whoops and wails, and Eddie rubs out animalistic noises on his guitar strings before raining down massive chord chunks. And while the largely ad-libbed lyrics are mostly nonsensical ("I took a mobile light, lookin' for a moonbeam"), the chorus is as direct and forceful as it gets. As Eddie said of the song's massive sound, "I just turn it up. Everything is on 10."

13
ICE CREAM MAN
`VAN HALEN`

IN HIS PRE–Van Halen days, DLR used to perform this horny midcentury blues— originally by John Brim— in solo acoustic form. It became a VH staple early on, before being recorded for posterity on the band's 1978 debut. And while Dave's vocals and acoustic guitar (tuned to open E) are a highlight of the studio version, Ed made sure to firebomb the proceedings with one of his most electrifying solos on record.

14
TAKE YOUR WHISKEY HOME
`WOMEN AND CHILDREN FIRST`

THIS THROBBING, mid-tempo cut is distinctive in the DLR-era VH catalog for how positively restrained the band sounds. Roth sticks mainly to his lower register, floating somewhere between singing and speaking the lyrics, while Eddie weaves a snakelike single-note riff around the rhythm section's incessant and steady thud. But this is Van Halen, of course, so there are still a few fireworks: a nimble and bluesy acoustic-guitar-and-vocal intro, and two quick but deadly EVH solo spots.

KERRY KING → "SEEING VAN HALEN LIVE MADE ME WANT TO PLAY. Eddie was the sh*t. I saw them six times on their first U.S. tour."

15
D.O.A.
`VAN HALEN II`

BY COMBINING Eddie Cochran teenage blues, Tom Waits gutter grit and one-chord punk-rock raunch, Van Halen created a poetic anthem of untamed youth that's the aural equivalent of a Fifties juvenile-delinquent exploitation film. Ed's acrobatic solo ascends, dives and spins out of control like a stunt pilot and ends with him wiggling an obnoxious mocking melody with his whammy bar, like a stiff middle finger waved under a police officer's nose.

ROSS HALFIN (VAN HALEN); JIMMY HUBBARD (KERRY KING)

16

ATOMIC PUNK

VAN HALEN

EDDIE OFTEN CREDITED Black Sabbath as an early influence, and you can really hear that inspiration during this song's verses when he plays rapid-fire staccato eighth notes that evoke "Paranoid." But Tony Iommi never played anything as brutally boisterous as Ed's intro, where he summoned a wash of dissonant white noise by rubbing the strings with his palm and processing the signal with an MXR Phase 90, creating what sounds like a helicopter with chainsaws for rotor blades.

SLASH → "I realized that even though I never tried to imitate Eddie, I do have a knack for going for the same kind of fast, fluid passages he does—which I obviously picked up subconsciously from listening to Van Halen records."

FIN COSTELLO/REDFERNS/GETTY IMAGES (VAN HALEN); TRAVIS SHINN (SLASH)

17
PUSH COMES TO SHOVE
FAIR WARNING

ALTHOUGH EDDIE says that "Push Comes to Shove" "was Roth's idea of trying to cash in on the reggae thing," it's really more of a slow, grinding funk song, thanks to Michael Anthony's disco bass line, Alex's steady drumming and Eddie's chorus-processed rhythms that slink instead of skank. The solo, however, veers into jazz-fusion territory as Eddie unleashes smooth legato lines reminiscent of Allan Holdsworth and palm-muted melodic runs à la Al Di Meola.

18
LITTLE GUITARS
DIVER DOWN 1982

THE TITLE REFERS to the miniature Les Paul replica built by Nashville luthier David Petschulat that Eddie used to record the song, which gave the guitar parts a distinctive, bright tone. Even cooler is the way Ed plucks chordal figures on several strings simultaneously to create a choppy, gated effect similar to what Pete Townshend played on "Won't Get Fooled Again," but Ed used only his fingers instead of an organ processed through a synthesizer.

19
JAMIE'S CRYIN'
VAN HALEN

ONE OF THE few songs on the first album that was written in the studio, this pop-friendly track also features one of the album's few overdubbed solos. The juicy midrange rhythm tone came from a korina Ibanez Destroyer, which Eddie said "was a great-sounding guitar—until I took a chunk out of it to make it look different. On the cover of *Women and Children First*, it's missing a piece. Boy, did I screw it up."

20
DIRTY MOVIES
FAIR WARNING

DLR SPINS A seedy tale of a prom-queen-turned-porn-queen, and Eddie matches him with a suitably lewd-sounding guitar melody—only his second slide performance (after "Could This Be Magic?") on a VH record. Eddie cut the song on a modified Gibson SG, which underwent further alteration during the recording sessions. When the guitar's bottom horn impeded his ability to reach the uppermost frets with his slide, he recalled, "I took a hacksaw right there in the studio and sawed it off."

21
SOMEBODY GET ME A DOCTOR
VAN HALEN II

THOUGH IT DIDN'T appear on record until *Van Halen II*, "Somebody Get Me a Doctor" dates back to the band's club days and appears on the demo (with the intro chords reversed) that they recorded with Gene Simmons in 1976. In addition to a riff that's as funky as anything in the EVH catalog, Ed offers up a solo that is positively blazing. Just how blazing? At its conclusion you can actually hear him get a round of applause from the band.

22
SPANISH FLY
VAN HALEN II

"ERUPTION" TURNED THE rock guitar world on its head. So what did EVH do for an encore? He unleashed another acrobatic, tap-infused shredfest—on acoustic guitar. A jaw-dropping performance, "Spanish Fly" had modest origins. Ed was "fooling around" on an acoustic when producer Ted Templeman "walked in and said 'You can play acoustic?' I looked at him like, What's the difference? It's got six strings! I ended up coming up with 'Spanish Fly.'"

23

JUMP
1984

EDDIE PREVIOUSLY played synthesizer on songs like "One Foot out the Door" and "Dancing in the Street," but here he plays his Oberheim OB-Xa like a true keyboard instrument instead of a surrogate guitar. "Certain people didn't want me playing keyboards because they thought I should only be a guitar hero," he recalled. "But hey, I'll play a Bavarian cheese whistle, if I can play it well—whatever that is." Ed calls his guitar solo—spliced from two separate takes—his favorite solo he never wrote.

24

LITTLE DREAMER
VAN HALEN

THIS LIVE STAPLE of the group's early days shows the polish and comfort of a road-tested tune. David Lee Roth gets the chance to prove he can do more than just wail, squeal and leap around as the band's hyperactive frontman—on this track, he shows he can actually *sing.* Eddie offers some attention-grabbing rapid-fire pull-offs in the solo, but he clearly steps back and helps create a midtempo, brooding groove so Dave can have the spotlight.

25

WOMEN IN LOVE...
VAN HALEN II

ALONG WITH THE same album's "Spanish Fly," the unaccompanied guitar intro to "Women in Love..." is a rare early documentation of EVH's stunning technique stripped of amp distortion. The 30 seconds of clean-toned, tap-harmonic-infused lines display yet another tool in the guitarist's seemingly bottomless arsenal, while the song's lyrics detail a rare instance in which David Lee Roth actually *loses* the girl...but at least it's to another girl.

ZAKK WYLDE
↓

"The first time I heard 'Spanish Fly,' I was like, HOW CAN SOMEBODY PLAY THE GUITAR THAT GOOD?"

26

ROMEO DELIGHT
WOMEN AND CHILDREN FIRST

SOME OF THE rhythm and lyric elements of this *Women and Children First* track were lifted from an earlier VH tune, "Get the Show on the Road," which appeared on their 1977 Warner Bros. demo. Though the song is a scorching rocker, it also features some more subtle ingredients, such as the incessant "heartbeat" sound heard during the verses and breakdown. Explained Eddie, "Mike was picking quietly, and I tapped my strings against the pickup poles."

27

SO THIS IS LOVE?
FAIR WARNING

"I DEFINITELY HAD a lot of pissed-off energy in me that I got out on *Fair Warning,*" Eddie admits. "It does have kind of a dark underlying tone to it." So why is this tasty piece of ear candy the only VH song that can legitimately be called "jaunty"? Credit Michael Anthony—this strutter positively bounces on the bass line, flowing into a smooth groove that finds the band thoroughly in the moment.

NEIL ZLOZOWER/ATLASICONS.COM (VAN HALEN); JIMMY HUBBARD (WYLDE)

CHRIS BRODERICK ↓
"EDDIE VAN HALEN WAS THE GUY ALL OF MY FRIENDS AND I WANTED TO BE."

ROSS HALFIN

28
TOP JIMMY
1984

DURING THE EARLY Eighties David Lee Roth frequented a notorious Hollywood after-hours club/art gallery called Zero Zero, where he commiserated with a bohemian crowd of lowbrow artists, models, underground filmmakers and punk rockers. Here he met rhythm 'n' booze singer Top Jimmy of Top Jimmy & the Rhythm Pigs, who passed away in 2001 but remains immortal thanks to this song. Ed used a DADACD tuning and played a Ripley stereo guitar with individual strings panned left or right in an alternating fashion.

29
RIGHT NOW
FOR UNLAWFUL CARNAL KNOWLEDGE

EDDIE WROTE THIS with Joe Cocker in mind, thinking the band might use guest vocalists after Dave's departure. It was a massive commercial hit with Sammy instead, using a dramatic piano riff borrowed from Eddie's soundtrack to the 1984 teen flick *The Wild Life*. The addition of a Hammond organ–Leslie speaker combo made for a key-heavy anthem that "some people thought was risky," Eddie says, "but to me, it's not even stepping out. It's still a rock tune."

30
WHERE HAVE ALL THE GOOD TIMES GONE!
DIVER DOWN

DAVID LEE ROTH once said that Van Halen learned six Kinks songs from a K-Tel greatest-hits album, but this song and "You Really Got Me" are their only Kinks covers that have surfaced. Considering the dearth of original songs on *Diver Down*, Van Halen probably should have retitled the song "Where Have All Our Good Tunes Gone!" but they still managed to deliver a spirited performance even if their revision of this Kinks classic wasn't as earth shattering as "You Really Got Me."

PAUL GILBERT
↓

"The legato playing that I do is very intuitive, and I learned it through a lot of good accidents. I used to sit around and play to Eddie Van Halen, **DOING IT WRONG AND COMING UP WITH MY OWN PATTERNS.**"

31
I'M THE ONE
`VAN HALEN`

AT ITS CORE "I'm the One" is a hot-rodded blues boogie tune that provided a springboard for Eddie to show off his impressive shredding chops, with a jazz scat vocal harmony interlude thrown in for comic relief. The true inspiration for Joe Satriani's "Satch Boogie" starts here, as Satriani copped everything, from Alex's thundering double-kick shuffle to Eddie's ascending triplet runs. Numerous shredders followed suit, but none were able to swing quite like Ed did here.

32
WHEN IT'S LOVE
`OU812`

THE FIRST SONG written for *5150*—hearing the music in the car en route from the airport, Sammy Hagar penned the lyrics before they reached the studio—Eddie called this unabashed power ballad "a classic tune" in 1988. "It's pretty, it's heavy, it's melodic, it's singalong...it's just a happening song." Ed, who has always cited Eric Clapton as a major influence, intended this song's solo as an overt tribute to Slowhand's style.

33
I'LL WAIT
`1984`

THOUGH "JUMP" IS the *1984* cut commonly credited with igniting the "to-keyboard-or-not-to-keyboard" rift in the VH camp, it was actually "I'll Wait" that, as Eddie recounted, David Lee Roth and producer Ted Templeman "didn't want to touch with a 10-foot pole." And indeed, whereas "Jump" is a guitar-based rocker at heart, "I'll Wait" is pure synth-pop, with Alex Van Halen on Rototoms and a co-writer credit for ex–Doobie Brother crooner Michael McDonald to boot.

34
GIRL GONE BAD
`1984`

DRAMATIC AND dynamic, "Girl Gone Bad" is the closest thing Van Halen ever recorded to a progressive rock epic, with Ed and Alex interlocking with stunning, nearly psychic precision to create a mammoth wall of sound. Ed's virtuoso guitar performance is like a condensed encyclopedia of his signature techniques, incorporating chiming harmonics, expansive open-string textures, melodic chord figures, brutal riffs, tremolo picking, tapping, squeals and dive bombs, but his "outside" jazzy flourishes may be the most impressive aspect of his tour de force solo.

FIN COSTELLO/REDFERNS/GETTY IMAGES (VAN HALEN); NEIL ZLOZOWER/ATLASICONS.COM (GILBERT)

35

5150

5150

AFTER HEARING THE rapid-fire double-stops and cascading drums that fill the first full minute of "5150," you'll wonder why Van Halen didn't just carry on as an instrumental trio. To his credit, Sammy squeals his highest note ever on the outro, but Eddie's solo is a stronger musical statement: a glorious 32-bar showcase of pure six-string skills. Let the man play all the synths he wants; this title track is his gift to his guitar fans.

36

CATHEDRAL

DIVER DOWN

PLENTY OF GUITARISTS (most notably David Gilmour, The Edge, Albert Lee and Grady Martin) had exploited the dotted-eighth-note-echo trick previously, but Eddie gave the effect a new twist by playing his quarter-note figures with volume-control swells, which, combined with cavernous hall-reverb processing, made his guitar sound like an organ. The first of three brief instrumental interludes on *Diver Down*, "Cathedral" stands alone as a complete musical piece instead of functioning as an extended song intro.

37

SINNER'S SWING!

FAIR WARNING

"THAT WAS spontaneous, a first take," Eddie says. That in-the-moment intensity is clear on the final product, as is some of the *Fair Warning* in-studio anxiety. An aggravated groove constantly shoves the song forward. Dave's urgent vocals suggest a lothario on the prowl, and Ed's frantic, slightly sloppy solo feels more like a panic attack, with rapid-fire tapping and hammer-ons barely constrained by six high-tension wires.

38

FEEL YOUR LOVE TONIGHT

VAN HALEN

DURING THE EIGHTIES countless hair metal pop hits copied this song's formula verbatim, from

GENE SIMMONS
↓

"While we were recording *Creatures of the Night*, I had lunch with Eddie. I can remember him pouring his heart out about how unhappy he was in Van Halen, and **EVENTUALLY HE ASKED US IF HE COULD JOIN KISS!"**

Roth's horny lyrics to the guitar-and-vocals-only breakdown during the choruses. However, none of the imitations equaled this song's lurid depiction of teenage lust, which was more effective than a cocktail of Spanish fly and Quaaludes for luring young lovelies into backseat action. Those of us who came of age during the Seventies pity today's teenagers with their Justin Bieber and Black Eyed Peas. It's a wonder anyone gets laid these days.

39

HANG 'EM HIGH

DIVER DOWN

THE WARNER BROS. demo track "Last Night" had to wait five years before it made the cut for *Diver Down*, trading its lame lyrics about a suspicious boyfriend for one of Dave's obtuse fables of danger and machismo. The reworked track is far more interesting, but Eddie's solo was almost identical in both versions, right down to the mid-solo key change, hammer-on trills and whammy workout.

40

(OH) PRETTY WOMAN

DIVER DOWN

EDDIE CAME UP with the idea to record a cover version of this early Sixties Roy Orbison hit when Van Halen's record label pressured them for a single after the *Fair Warning* tour. Eddie liked its riff, but much to his chagrin, the song became the band's biggest hit, despite being one of only two Van Halen songs to that date without a guitar solo. "It shows you how much guitar solos mean to people," he lamented later.

TIME & LIFE PICTURES/GETTY IMAGES (VAN HALEN); TRAVIS SHINN (SIMMONS)

41
ONE FOOT OUT THE DOOR
FAIR WARNING

FAIR WARNING'S CLOSING track was reportedly recorded on the quick, when the band literally had one foot out the door of the studio. Built on an ominous, burbling synth line carried over from the album's previous track, the instrumental "Sunday Afternoon in the Park," the song is a bare-bones rocker that flies by in a mere 1:58. Even better, more than half of that time is taken up by a furious EVH solo.

45
SHE'S THE WOMAN
A DIFFERENT KIND OF TRUTH

AFTER RECORDING THREE demo versions of this song—an early self-produced take, one with Gene Simmons in 1976 and another with Ted Templeman in 1977—Van Halen finally released an official studio version of "She's the Woman" on the new album *A Different Kind of Truth*. Since Ed had already lifted the original solo section and used it in "Mean Street," he wrote a new one that, in addition to the intro's cool chromatic bass figure, really allows his son, bassist Wolfgang, to strut his stuff.

46
DANCING IN THE STREET
DIVER DOWN

ED PLAYED THIS song's riff on a Minimoog synthesizer processed with the same dotted-eighth note echo effect he used on "Cathedral"—"two songs I couldn't have done without an echo," he admits. "The riff was taken from a song of my own that I was in the midst of writing. Ted [*Templeman*] heard it and said, 'Hey, let's use it for 'Dancing in the Street.' Maybe if I played it on guitar on the record it would have been better."

42
TATTOO
A DIFFERENT KIND OF TRUTH
2012

"TATTOO" IS BASED on an early VH tune titled "Down in Flames" that was slated to appear on *Van Halen II*. Instead it emerged—with new lyrics, solo and other pieces—34 years later as the leadoff single from the new *A Different Kind of Truth*. The result is a comfortable and welcome link between VH past and present. And take note of the guitar swells at the song's coda, which did actually make it onto *VH II*—as the intro to that album's "You're No Good."

43
FINISH WHAT YA STARTED
OU812 1988

WITH ITS TWANGY finger-style guitar, dry drums and lyrics about blue balls, "Finish What Ya Started" is easily the most un–Van Halen song in the band's catalog. Alex plunks on a kit that sounds like tuna cans as Eddie performs finger-lickin' chicken-pickin' lines on a Fender Stratocaster plugged directly into the mixing console. Sammy's lyrics actually make sense for once, as it's easy to imagine a woman stopping him in the act when she realizes she's having sex with Sammy Hagar.

44
WHY CAN'T THIS BE LOVE
5150

RELEASED IN MARCH 1986 as the first single from *5150*, "WCTBL" was for most people the first music heard from the Hagar-led Van Halen. And indeed, the song's bright, bouncy and downright pop sound, which features Eddie playing an Oberheim OB-8 synth, made it clear that, yeah, they were serious about that keyboard thing. How serious, you ask? When VH performed this song live in the Eighties, Eddie would often stick to the keys and leave the guitar rhythms—and solo—to Sammy.

47
POUNDCAKE
FOR UNLAWFUL CARNAL KNOWLEDGE
1991

THE MASSIVE GUITAR sound on this cut is the result of Ed overdubbing three rhythm parts: his main six-string, and two tracks of electric 12-string, for which he played a custom model built by English luthier Roger Giffin. Combined with the cascades of guitar harmonics that ring throughout, a white-hot solo spot and an intro played with the assistance of a Makita power drill, "Poundcake" announced that EVH was still a major guitar force to be reckoned with.

NEIL ZLOZOWER/ATLASICONS.COM

48
TOP OF THE WORLD
FOR UNLAWFUL CARNAL KNOWLEDGE

THE OPENING RIFF sound familiar? That's because it's more or less the same one Ed played almost a decade earlier on the fadeout to *1984*'s "Jump." Legend has it that Eddie didn't want "TOTW" included on *For Unlawful Carnal Knowledge*, preferring to focus on fresher material. Producer Andy Johns convinced him otherwise, but not before Eddie could pull out another blast from the past—he recorded the song using the '58 Gibson Flying V he played on another *1984* hit, "Hot for Teacher."

49
BEST OF BOTH WORLDS
5150

THIS *5150* **TRACK,** featuring a wide-open cowboy-chord riff that sounds like AC/DC playing Kool & the Gang's "Celebration," is one of the most well-known cuts of the Hagar era. A live version, lifted from the 1986 *Live Without a Net* home video, was a minor hit on MTV, allowing viewers who couldn't make it to the show the opportunity to witness Sam, Ed and Mike march in line formation—and Day-Glo pants— across the concert stage.

50
DANCE THE NIGHT AWAY
VAN HALEN II

"DANCE THE NIGHT AWAY" was reportedly inspired by Fleetwood Mac's "Go Your Own Way," and indeed, the song is one of the few pure pop tunes of the DLR era. As such, the emphasis is heavily on the vocals and chorus harmonies (the title refrain was originally "Dance Lolita Dance," until Roth was convinced otherwise). Though Eddie's guitar is uncharacteristically restrained (no solo!), he still contributes some stellar harmonics work and a classic major-chord riff.

NEIL ZLOZOWER/ATLASICONS.COM

ATOMIC PUNK

The story of how Eddie Van Halen revolutionized rock guitar.

- - - - -

by Dan Amrich

SOME SOUNDS ARE UNMISTAKABLE. Some are undefinable. More often than not, Van Halen is both. // Now, 25 years after catching the world's ear and shaking it violently, the aftershocks of Edward Van Halen's explosive guitar technique, radical ideas and boundless energy are still being felt. Surviving disco, punk, power pop, grunge and countless other trends, Eddie has proven himself as the ultimate—if somewhat reluctant—rock guitar hero.

Edward Lodewijk Van Halen was born on January 26, 1957, in Nijmegen, Holland. He and his elder brother Alex moved with their musician parents to Pasadena, California, when he was 10 years old. The family had 15 dollars and a piano, and what little of the former the family had went into teaching the children how to play the latter. But while Eddie respected the instrument, learned a lot about music in general and won numerous awards for his keyboard prowess, his heart wasn't in it. "Who wanted to sit at the piano?" he later said. "I wanted to go crazy!"

As American teens, Alex and Eddie learned both the English language and the language of rock and roll. Eddie invested in drums and

Alex got a nylon-string acoustic guitar; while Eddie was busy delivering papers to pay for his kit, Alex was busy using it. Once Alex mastered "Wipeout," Eddie told Alex to keep the drums; he'd take the guitar. Both parties were happy. As Alex later recalled, "I could tell by the way he was moving his fingers around that he could do things I'd never be able to do, no matter how hard I practiced."

What he did with that guitar ultimately changed the face of rock, but in the early days, it was essentially just a case of jamming with his brother (using a Tiesco Del Rey electric guitar from Sears) and listening to a lot of early Beatles, Dave Clark Five, Jimi Hendrix, Jimmy Page and especially Eric Clapton, whose licks he learned note

ROSS HALFIN

The recording of *Van Halen II* at Sunset Sound in Hollywood, 1978.

"Eruption" was nothing less than pure rock guitar revolution.

for note. Eventually, Eddie and Alex played covers at high school events with an endless stream of temporary bassists, under the name Mammoth—"a junior Cream," said Eddie. Yet the more he played, the more he realized he wanted to take his playing to the next level, beyond mere mimicry and into innovation.

But before anyone could hear Eddie's ideas, some basic problems had to be solved: primarily, finding a place to practice and finding cash to pay for a P.A. system during live gigs. Both were solved when David Lee Roth joined the band; the Van Halens had been renting Roth's equipment occasionally, and Roth's dad let them practice in the basement. The fact that Roth's extroverted antics garnered the band a lot of attention didn't hurt. When Michael Anthony gave up his own band, Snake, to play bass for Mammoth in 1974, the group became the hottest ticket in Pasadena. It wasn't too long after that they realized that Mammoth was the name of another band in the area, so Roth suggested they be known as simply Van Halen. "It had power to it," he said. Nobody could come up with anything better, so it stuck.

Playing mostly covers for five hours a night at various Southern California clubs, Eddie's technique inevitably mutated and, before long, local guitarists were heading to shows to check out his raw sound, homemade guitars and unorthodox technique of using two hands on the fretboard. Eddie, meanwhile, took his brother's advice and played solos with his back to the audience, so nobody could rip him off. As time wore on, the band got better gigs, working at leg-

endary L.A. clubs like the Whisky and the Starwood, added more and more original material and, in 1977, caught the ear of Kiss bassist Gene Simmons. Simmons was impressed from note one and helped the band—then calling itself Daddy Longlegs—record a professional demo which was promptly rejected by every major label. It wasn't until Warner Bros. producer Ted Templeman personally convinced the label's president, Mo Ostin, to go see a VH show that the band got signed.

In February 1978, Van Halen's Templeman-produced, self-titled first album was released. An unholy wail of car horns assaulted listeners as "Runnin' with the Devil" kicked off the record, but it was merely a warning shot; the following track, "Eruption," was nothing less than pure rock guitar revolution. Pinch harmonics, hammer-ons, two-handed tapping, whammy bar dives so deep they'll give you the bends—all in one terrifying package. As the guitar world scratched its collective head and tried to figure out what the hell had just happened, Edward Van Halen had altered the very perception of what rock guitar was—in one minute, 42 seconds flat.

On the combined strengths of "Runnin' with the Devil," a high-octane cover of the Kinks' "You Really Got Me" and Ed's jaw-dropping calisthenics, *Van Halen* cracked the Top 20 and sold two million copies in a matter of months. Opening nationwide tours for acts like Montrose and Journey, the band quickly cemented a backstage reputation of babes, booze and bad behavior, spearheaded in no small part by Roth. Onstage, however, Van Halen was all business,

NEIL ZLOZOWER/ATLASICONS.COM

NEIL ZLOZOWER/ATLASICONS.COM

pounding out adrenaline-soaked half-hour sets to stunned audiences. By the time they opened for Black Sabbath in Europe, the changing of the heavy rock guard was evident. "They blew us off the stage every night," recalled Ozzy Osbourne. "It was so embarrassing. We didn't have the fire anymore. They kicked our asses, but it convinced me of two things: my days with Black Sabbath were over, and Van Halen was going to be a very successful band."

By that December, the band had recorded a second album, cleverly titled *Van Halen II*. "Dance the Night Away" hit Number 15, holding its own against the disco fare of the time and, by June 1979, the band was the headline act of a U.K. tour, with 22 tons of equipment in tow. Songs like "Beautiful Girls" helped solidify David Lee Roth's party persona, while the nylon-string solo "Spanish Fly" was Eddie's proof that daring moves need not be performed on an electric.

By 1980, Van Halen had helped fuel a heavy metal resurgence—though Eddie was uncomfortable with the phrase "heavy metal" to

characterize the band. David Lee Roth, meanwhile, described Van Halen's music as "a cross between religion and hockey." Still, the group's third album, *Women and Children First*, oozed distorted riffs and thundering drums, ultimately hitting number nine on the *Billboard* album chart. It also contained decidedly non-metallic gems like the acoustic slide number "Could This Be Magic?" previous to which Eddie had never played slide guitar.

While on that year's "Invasion" tour, Eddie met TV actress Valerie Bertinelli and their romance blossomed quickly; the two were married in April 1981. It's ironic, then, that in the wake of one of Eddie's happiest moments, the band released its darkest album, *Fair Warning*. Creepy synth-driven pieces like "Sunday Afternoon in the Park" and the sordid subject matter of "Mean Street" and "Dirty Movies" ultimately overshadowed party rockers like "Unchained" and "So This Is Love?" But despite the fact that the lead single, "So This Is Love?" only reached Number 115 on the *Billboard* chart, the album still charted higher than any of its predecessors, reaching number six.

Bending to record company pressures, the band recorded their fifth album, *Diver Down*, in 12 days to meet an April 1982 release date. The record clocked in at under 30 minutes and contained five cover tunes within its 12 tracks, a fact that didn't sit well with Eddie. "That's my least favorite record," he said later. "I'd rather bomb with my own songs than make it with someone else's." Still, the album isn't without its gems, particularly the volume-knob trickery of "Cathedral," the Spanish-style intro to "Little Guitars" and the guest appearance of Eddie and Alex's dad, Jan Van Halen, playing clarinet on "Big Bad Bill (Is Sweet William Now)." Warner Bros. was no doubt happy, as the album soared to Number Three and the "Hide Your Sheep" tour kicked off at the mammoth 1982 US Festival in California.

But the tour was short and Eddie found himself with some welcome downtime at home. Unexpectedly, producer Quincy Jones called up and asked Eddie to contribute a solo to a new song for Michael Jackson's upcoming album, *Thriller*. It was generally frowned upon for Van Halen members to work outside of the band

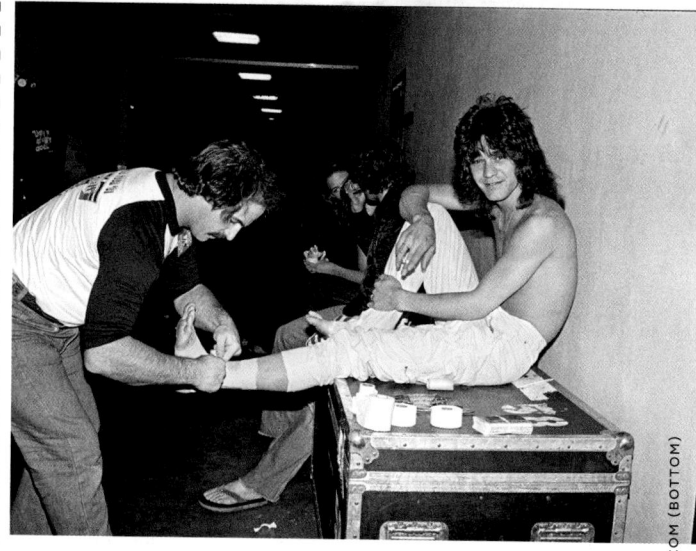

(although Eddie had previously contributed to Nicolette Larson's *Nicolette* and Brian May's *Star Fleet Project*), but since his bandmates were all out on various vacations, Eddie agreed. After requesting a different section of the song to solo over, Ed cut two takes in 20 minutes. "Beat It" spent three weeks at Number One and, largely due to Eddie's solo, crossed over to radio stations that normally wouldn't play R&B artists. *Thriller* went on to be the biggest-selling album of all time; Eddie, meanwhile, received a thank-you note and no payment, having done the solo as a favor.

While Roth later sniffed that "I ain't heard anything different," the "Beat It" favor was ultimately returned by listeners when *1984* was released on New Year's Eve, 1983. The leadoff single, "Jump," hit Number One in late February and stayed there for five weeks—to date, it's the band's only chart-topping hit. The fact that the guitar god's biggest hit was driven by a synthesizer hook seemed to bother

MARK WEISS (TOP); NEIL ZLOZOWER/ATLASICONS.COM (BOTTOM)

everyone but Eddie; to him, it was just music. After all, the guy *did* have a classical piano background. Besides, the guitar faithful were rewarded with *1984*'s "Panama," "Top Jimmy" and the raucous "Hot for Teacher."

But widespread pop success came with a price. While David Lee Roth lapped up the attention, Eddie was thinking ahead to the next record. Roth had always preferred life on the road to life in a sound-booth and eventually their personal and work ethic differences came to a head. Roth had tasted solo success with his *Crazy from the Heat* album and, by June 1985, announced he was leaving the band. Ted Templeman went with him, leaving the producing duties to long-time engineer Donn Landee and the increasingly involved Eddie.

As a replacement for the acrimoniously departed Roth, the band considered doing the next album with a different lead singer on every track, but abandoned the idea after auditioning Sammy Hagar, ex-Montrose vocalist and solo artist in his own right. Hagar's fresh energy and more agreeable personality fueled 1986's *5150*, produced by Landee, the band and Mick Jones. Despite open skepticism over the missing Roth, the album became the band's first Number One record, spawning two keyboard-heavy hits, "Why Can't This Be Love" and "Dreams" as well as strong guitar rockers like "Best of Both Worlds" and some wild Steinberger antics on "Get Up." Eddie later referred to it as "a very inspired record" with "a lot of soul."

Two years of vacation later, the band headlined the Monsters of Rock tour in the summer of 1988, playing all-day concerts alongside Metallica and the Scorpions, and released the second Hagar-fronted record, *OU812*, in June. With fans eager for new material, it captured the top spot on the album charts in under a month, sitting there for four weeks. "When It's Love," "Finish What Ya Started" and "Feels So Good" all enjoyed heavy radio airplay.

After the grueling tour, the band enjoyed some well-earned R&R. In 1990, the band opened their own club, the Cabo Wabo Cantina, in Cabo San Lucas, Mexico. The next year, on March 16, 1991, Eddie and Valerie gave birth to their first son, Wolfgang William Van Halen. With another partner, Eddie soon gave birth to another child: the Ernie Ball Music Man guitar he helped design. For a tinkerer like Eddie, creating a production instrument was the ultimate thrill. "I used to endorse the guitar I played," he said, "but I designed this one. It's a whole different ballgame."

Following closely behind the new ax came a new Andy Johns–produced album, *For Unlawful Carnal Knowledge*, in June 1991. The lead single, "Poundcake," continued Ed's tradition of making weird noises with guitars thanks to its electric drill opening hook while "Top of the World" picks up where "Jump" left off—literally, as it uses the "Jump" outro as its opening riff. Although the piano-based "Right Now" turned into a huge hit, the album seemed more guitar-oriented than recent efforts, staying at the Number One spot on the album charts for three weeks.

Although Eddie had said in 1985 that he "didn't see the purpose" of a live album, he eventually changed his mind for *Right Here, Right Now*, released in February 1993. The band's first two-CD set featured material from the latest tour, a bass solo, a drum solo, lots of stage chatter from Hagar and a live solo by Eddie that encompasses "Eruption," "Cathedral," "316" and countless wild squeals. The

MARTY TEMME/WIREIMAGE/ GETTY IMAGES

album also featured Eddie's new Peavey 5150 amplifiers.

By the end of 1994, Eddie had severed his ties with Music Man, opting instead to evolve his earlier design for his amp manufacturer as the Peavey Wolfgang. More importantly, Eddie had stopped drinking and found that writing was far easier when he was sober. The appropriately named *Balance* debuted in January of the following year, ranging from the commercially poppy "Can't Stop Lovin' You" to the power boogie of "Big Fat Money" and no less than three instrumentals, reportedly due to difficulty getting Hagar to write lyrics. The album continued the band's Number One streak, holding the top spot for a week.

But within six months, Hagar would be history, leaving the group following disputes over the planned greatest-hits albums and the band's contributions to the *Twister* soundtrack (neatly summed up as "creative differences"). "We actually had problems on every album except for *5150*," Eddie revealed later. With Hagar's departure, old-school fans hoped beyond hope that a reunion with David

Lee Roth was in the future—and it was, albeit for just two new songs for 1996's *Best of Volume 1*, "Me Wise Magic" and "Can't Get This Stuff No More." With "Magic" as its single, *Best Of* nailed *Billboard*'s top album spot, but almost as soon as the original lineup started feeling each other out, a disastrous backstage ego flareup at the MTV Video Music Awards squelched all hopes of future involvements between the band and Roth. "I'll put it very simply," said Eddie. "Dave and Sam both suffer from L.S.D.—lead singer's disease."

"Gary's very talented, and we work very, very well together," said Eddie of Van Halen's third singer, former Extreme vocalist Gary Cherone.

With Cherone on board, *Van Halen III* was, as its title suggests, a new beginning for the band, and a major milestone—the first track was called "Neuworld" for a reason. Liberated from drugs, alcohol and various other physical and mental restraints, Eddie spoke in interviews passionately about his muse, his new approach to writing and recording music, as well as his emotional and spiritual rebirth.

Featuring Ed on six-string bass as well as electric sitar, the experimental album was released in February 1998, debuting at Number Four on the album charts and powered by the single "Without You." However, many fans disliked the band's new direction and the album stalled.

Dark times for Van Halen quickly followed. Almost everything that could go wrong for Eddie did. The band parted ways with Cherone in November 1999. "I had a great time singing with the band and I wish Eddie, Alex and Michael all the best," said Cherone in a statement. The band had been working on a new album with producers Patrick Leonard and Danny Kortchmar; the results of those sessions will likely never see release.

By May 2000, rumors were flying that Eddie, a longtime smoker, was battling tongue cancer. Close to a year later, Van Halen confirmed the rumors on the band's web site. "I'm sorry for having waited so long to address this issue personally, but cancer can

With Gary Cherone in Mountain View, CA, on July 5, 1998

AL PEREIRA/MICHAEL OCHS ARCHIVES/GETTY IMAGES (TOP); TIM MOSENFELDER/IMAGEDIRECT/GETTY IMAGES (BOTTOM)

be a very unique and private matter to deal with. I was examined by three oncologists and three head and neck surgeons at Cedars Sinai just before spring break and I was told that I'm healthier than ever and beating cancer. Although it's hard to say when, there's a good chance I will be cancer-free in the near future. I just want to thank all of you for your concern and support. Love, Eddie." By May 2002, Ed reported that he'd "gotten a 100-percent clean bill of health—from head to toe"—but his 21-year marriage to Valerie Bertinelli was not so lucky, ultimately ending in July 2002. To make matters worse, Warner Bros. very quietly had dropped the band from its artist roster some months earlier. After more than 70 million albums sold worldwide, one of the all-time great rock and roll bands found itself homeless.

Then, impossibly, David Lee Roth and Sammy Hagar joined forces for a tour together in the summer of 2002. Humbly titled Song for Song: The Heavyweight Champs of Rock and Roll Tour (but nicknamed the "Sans Halen" tour by fans), Sam and Dave played dates through September, with Dave dipping into the classic VH catalog more often than Sammy. "I'm not sure what the [*Van Halen*] brothers think, and I'm not sure I even really care," said Roth during

Sammy was coaxed back when Michael Anthony was allowed to tour, but only after Anthony agreed to take less money for the gig. But despite the lower fee, he still had to deal with the higher tensions. "There came a point to where we actually split it up and we traveled on two different jets; Eddie and Al would fly on one jet and Sammy and I would fly on another," he told *Burrn!* magazine in 2006. "This was only to keep the peace. It got to the point to where I couldn't even see this thing going on much longer without somebody blowing up. So Sammy finally said, 'I'm not doing any more dates because this is just not working.'"

That brief tour was the last time Michael Anthony would play with Van Halen. And while much has been made of the Eddie/Dave feud over the years, a *Diver Down*–era lost interview with Eddie surfaced in 2006, clearly illustrating that Eddie's disdain for Mike ran even deeper: "I won't rag too much on Dave; he pulls his weight. Mike doesn't. He doesn't do anything; he has no input whatsoever. But he has remodeled his whole house and bought himself a Turbo Carrera with the money he's made off us. Whatever."

In late 2006, Eddie made it official: Mike was officially out, and his 16-year-old son Wolfgang was Van Halen's new bassist. More news quickly followed that was almost as unbelievable: David Lee Roth was back as the lead singer, and the whole crew would be hitting the road in 2007. Unfortunately, that fire was quickly extinguished by news that Eddie had returned to rehab. It was necessary and Eddie was healthy within a few weeks, but the timing was terrible: Eddie retreated just four days before Van Halen was inducted into the Rock and Roll Hall of Fame. Alex, Dave, and Wolfgang did not attend the ceremony, leaving Sammy and Mike to awkwardly represent a band with which they were no longer on speaking terms. "I can't tell you how much I wish everyone was here tonight," said Sammy at the ceremony. "It's out of our control and it's out of some other people's control. I think Eddie's going to come

Michael Anthony onstage with Sammy Hagar in 2002.

the press blitz. "I think probably the two biggest words up there on Howdy Doody mountain now are 'Uh-oh.'" Dave's subsequent filing and dropping of a lawsuit against his former bandmates later in the year only seemed to dash hopes of an eventual reunion.

Sammy, however, sent mixed messages over the course of the summer, saying "Quite honestly, I'm not interested" to the Wisconsin *Journal Sentinel* in June but "I think a reunion is inevitable" at the MTV Video Music Awards three months later. Sure enough, by the fall of 2003, reunion rumors once again circulated, this time with Sammy at the lead, but the Van Halen camp kept silent, until finally announcing tour dates and a new band photo in March 2004. The tour was in support of the two-disc *Best of Both Worlds*, spearheaded by the appropriately titled Sammy-sung single, "It's About Time." But this "inevitable" reunion was also short-lived; as Sammy later revealed in an online interview with bullz-eye.com in 2008, things were difficult before the summer tour even started. "When I did the reunion in 2004, Eddie said he wanted to get a new bass player, and I thought he wasn't going to play with Mike. I said, 'Well, then you're going to get a new singer, too, dude.' I said 'bye' and I split."

out the other side a better person and maybe we'll all get our buddy back."

Eddie did return for the stadium tour in the fall, featuring a clean-cut spandex-free Roth strutting, dancing and twirling microphone stands like the frontman he was always born to be. Now 17, Wolfgang played a blue-black-and-white striped Fender Jazz bass onstage as a tribute to his dad, but only after several months of intense jam sessions and rehearsals that grew organically. "We didn't lay out a plan or anything," said Wolfgang in a *Guitar World* interview. "It just fell together. We played together a good four months without any vocals, and we just looked at each other and knew it was awesome." Ed, meanwhile, was one proud papa: "I couldn't wait for the day I'd be able to make music with my son. I don't know what more I could ask for."

How about your own brand? That same year, Fender debuted the EVH line of guitars and accessories, launching with a stunning replica of Eddie's red, white and black "Frankenstein" guitar. Every detail, from cigarette burns and rust to the 1971 quarter screwed into the body near the bridge, was reproduced with such accuracy that Ed himself

BARRY BRECHEISEN/WIREIMAGE/GETTY IMAGES

said he couldn't tell the difference. The irony of a $25,000 replica of a guitar that Eddie built for around $200 was not lost on guitar collectors, but the Frankenstein is more than an instrument—it's an icon.

After Sammy and Mike formed their own supergroup, Chickenfoot, with Red Hot Chili Peppers drummer Chad Smith and shred virtuoso Joe Satriani in 2009, all signs pointed to the Van Halen reunion being permanent. But was the most recent Roth tour just a nostalgic stage show, or was an album in the works as fans had hoped? Rumors swirled in 2010 that Eddie was hard at work on new material with fresh lyrics by Dave, and that the band was digging through the archives of unreleased tracks and old demos for suitable songs. After months of speculation that Sony would sign the band, Interscope officially announced they had landed Van Halen in late 2011, complete with a photo of band members posing with execs. A few days later, the Grammy Awards hinted heavily on Twitter that the band would perform at the nomination announcement concert, but it wasn't to be.

However, fans finally got the holiday present they'd been hoping for: a teaser posted the day after Christmas on the band's website confirmed a February album release and a 2012 tour. Sammy sniffed to *Rolling Stone* that the forthcoming album was "all old stuff," and he wasn't entirely wrong: *A Different Kind of Truth* featured several songs reworked or revived from the band's early club and demo days. "Let's Get Rockin' " became "Outta Space," "Big Trouble" changed to "Big River," "Put Out the Lights" was revised as "Beats Workin'," and the lead single, "Tattoo," was a reimagined version of "Down in Flames." One of Eddie's pieces from the *Wild Life* soundtrack, "Ripley," was reworked as "Blood and Fire," while two other songs from the club days, "She's the Woman" and "Bullethead," were simply presented with fresh arrangements and modern performances. The result is a strange, glorious hybrid: Modern sounds with classic vibes, fresh yet familiar. Ultimately, it makes sense: By going back to the beginning and reconciling with its own musical past, Van Halen really has started over.

World tours, roster changes, life-threatening illnesses, David Lee Roth—Van Halen, it seems, can survive anything. Having passed the 35-year mark, the band is less a mere musical group and more a simple force of nature: unpredictable, indestructible and undeniably powerful. At age 57, Eddie remains what he has always been: a master guitarist, supremely confident of his craft and his multiple role as songwriter, producer and musician. "I still have so much music in me," says Eddie. "So much that needs to come out." ◼

Wolfgang Van Halen (center) in Charlotte, NC, September 27, 2007.

KEVIN MAZUR/WIREIMAGE/GETTY IMAGES

KEVIN WINTER/GETTY IMAGES

I still have so much music in me.

—Eddie Van Halen

ROSS HALFIN

CALIFORNIA DREAMIN'

In this revealing interview conducted just a few weeks after the February 1978 release of *Van Halen*, Eddie Van Halen spoke out about his lifelong dreams of being a rock star.

by Steven Rosen

Was your father a musician?

Yeah, he got us into music very early. He got Al [*Alex Van Halen, Eddie's brother*] and me practicing piano for concert stuff, classical piano, at like seven and eight years old.

You were that young?

Oh, yeah. My brother was six, I think, when he started and I started when I was about seven. Then my family moved [*from the Netherlands*] to southern California and we started getting into rock and roll a little bit. The Dave Clark Five, the real early stuff. And I went out and got myself a paper route and bought a drum set. Originally I played drums and my brother played guitar.

Is that right?

While I was out throwin' my papers, he was practicing my drums. He got better than I did and I said, "Okay, you play my drums and I'll pick up your guitar." It went on from there. I'd say I really didn't start playing guitar and getting into lead guitar and stuff like that until Cream came out; when the heavy guitar thing started to happen.

Do you remember the first guitar you had?

Yeah. [*laughs*] A Sears Teisco Del Rey; a three-pickup job. I thought the more pickups and switches it had, the better guitar it was. Nowadays I've got kind of a homemade copy of a Strat with just one pickup and one volume knob. Really simple. It looks like a Strat but there's a place in San Dimas, California, called Charvel Guitars and they custom make 'em. Mine wasn't really custom made—it was like a junk neck and a hacked-up body that was just lying around and I wanted to experiment building my own guitar. So I could get the sound I wanted. See, I always wanted a Strat for the vibrato bar because I love that effect. So I just bought it from them for $50 and the neck for $90 and slapped it together. Put an old humbucking pickup in it and one volume knob and painted it up the way I wanted it to look and it screams. My main guitar up until right now.

I wanted to be a
rock and roll star.

Is that the black and white striped guitar?
Yeah—it's the one on the cover of the album. Just one pickup and one volume knob—no tone or fancy out-of-phase switches or nothin' like that.

You used to use a Fender Strat?
Yeah, but I couldn't get the sound I wanted out of a regular Strat. Somebody told me about the Charvel place and about their wood. Their bodies get much better tone and stuff like that, so I checked it out.

You only need the one volume control and the single pickup to get all the tone you need?
Yeah. I use a couple of effects, like an MXR phase shifter, a flanger and two Echoplexes, which change the sound a bit. And I use two Univox echo boxes also for the end of my solo on "Eruption." That's not an Echoplex; it's a Univox. Everything I use is MXR; it's about all I can afford. Mounted on a piece of wood. I use a pretty long cord onstage—about a 25- or a 30-footer, and after it goes through the pedals I use an equalizer to boost the line back up. But tone-wise I just crank everything all the way up and, depending on how you pick, you get different tones and stuff. My amp setup is pretty tricked though.

Tell me about your rig.
I've got six old Marshalls that have been rebuilt. They have bigger tubes in 'em and bigger transformers to make 'em a lot louder. I use six heads hooked to six cabinets. The cabinets are pretty much stock except I changed the way they look a little bit. And I use these things called voltage generators. What this box does is it enables me to crank up the voltage higher than the amp is supposed to take. It really makes the tubes red-hot, you know; it really makes the amp overload so much that it gets the sound I like.

Do you use any special settings on the Marshalls?
I just crank 'em all the way up—everything all the way up.

Do you use the same setup in the studio?
I use the exact same thing.

You actually crank up six Marshall stacks in the studio?
Oh, no, no no. [*laughs*] Okay, see, the thing is I get the exact same sound out of one or out of six. All the difference in numbers just means how loud it's gonna be. And each amp sounds the same. I use two actually because I like to feel it too while I'm playing.

It must be pretty loud in the studio.
Oh, yeah—we play at stage volume. We recorded at Sunset Sound... I like that room. It's just a big room—it's like our basement, actually. The guys who run the studio and maintain the place, they walk in after we're done, and there are beer cans all over the floor and Pink's hot dog smears all over the place. But in order for us to be comfortable we just do what we want.

How you do you manage to keep your guitar in tune with so much whammy bar stuff going on in your playing?
That is a very tricky question. So far I haven't told or showed anybody. I dicked around with a Strat for years learning how to do that and there's about four or five different things that you have to do, including knowing the technique of playing it. A lot of people just grab the bar and go wahwahwahwahwah [*mimics the sound of a bar going up and down*] and expect it to stay in tune. There are little things that you have to do, like after you hit the bar and you bring the note down, usually one of the strings goes sharp. So before you come back in with a full chord, you have to stretch with your left hand to pop it back. Without picking the string, you just grab the string and jerk it up real quick and then it pops right back to where it was before you hit the bar. And then on top of that, you know the little metal jobs at the top? What part of the guitar is that? I don't even know. Where the tuning pegs are, Fender always has these little metal things that hold the strings down. String retainers or whatever they're called. If you have those too tight, the string will get caught up on that and it won't pop back the way it's supposed to. Also, it's the way you wind your strings.

How do you wind your strings?
Hey, I don't know if I want to tell you! It's basically simple and the kind of strings you use is important. I use Fender strings—they're very good and I like 'em.

What gauges do you use?
They're pretty light, really: .040, .032, .024, .015, .011 and .009. So far for that Strat those are the best gauges for keeping it in tune. I used to think that the heavier strings I used, the better it would stay in

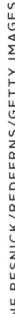

LORNE RESNICK/REDFERNS/GETTY IMAGES

RICHARD E. AARON/REDFERNS/GETTY IMAGES

tune, but that ain't true either.

Have you done anything to the tuning pegs themselves?
I use Schallers—they're not regular Fenders.

Have you played with the bridge?
The spring setup—they come with five springs and I only use four. It's hard to explain everything because it also depends on the guitar. I could tell you exactly what to do and you could do it to your Strat and it wouldn't work. And also there's a thing in the back where the strings hook up; there are two long screws and how tight you got that set, it changes the tension of the springs. So it's that—how you wind your strings, how many springs you got, the string retainers at the top and the way you play it. It took me a while to figure it out.

Do you think you'll stick with these Strat-styled guitars?
When we were in New Orleans, I just bought a Les Paul. I needed another guitar because I tend to bend the hell out of the strings a lot—usually after my solo live, I change guitars. So I needed another guitar and when we were in New Orleans I just picked up a Les Paul. It's a real nice white one.

Do you play any acoustic guitar?
I have never in my life owned an acoustic guitar; I really haven't. I've written songs on electric guitar that would sound real nice on an acoustic but I've never owned an acoustic guitar. I guess one of these days I'll buy one. I don't know anything about acoustics. I know what I like in electric guitars, but acoustic I'm lost. I don't know what's good.

Do you play any slide guitar?
A little bit; there's nothing on the record. There's no slide on the record. But who knows what lurks in the future? Me and my brother both play keyboards, too—I've been thinking about getting a synthesizer. But who knows? I might not.

Onstage (left) and backstage (below) in London on May 27, 1978.

out playing because I really liked to.

Do you still practice?
Sure. I mean, I've got a guitar right here in my hands right now. I change the strings before a gig; I play for half-an-hour, an hour, just to break in the strings and loosen up my fingers. And at night sometimes I come home and write a tune.

You change the strings before every gig?
Oh, yeah, every day—especially on the Strat; they wear out so quick with that bar.

Talking about the album, it really sounds like there isn't a lot of overdubbing going on.
Oh, no, no. I hate overdubbing because it's just not the same as playing with the guys—there's no feeling there for me to work off of. I've got to feed off them to play good, too. Like "Runnin' with the Devil" is a melodic solo, so I put a rhythm underneath it. Songs that have a spontaneous solo, like "I'm the One," "Ice Cream Man" and most of the songs on the album, Ted Templeman, our producer, felt that it was good enough on its own without fattening it up. Also, when we play it live, it sounds the same. I don't like it when bands over-produce in the studio and then when they play live it doesn't sound the same. With us it sounds exactly the same and maybe even better because you get to see us doing it at the same time. It's very energetic—we'll get you up and shake your ass.

Was Ted important in bringing out the best in you?
Oh, sure. What he managed to do was put our live sound on a record. I mean, a lot of people have to do a bunch of overdubs to make it sound full. It's a lot easier to make a lot of instruments sound full than a guitar, bass and drums. That's where Ted comes in—he knows his shit. He's the man. He's doing our next one, too.

You were pleased with your solos and the sound of your guitar on *Van Halen*?
It was cool. I'm not saying I couldn't do better, but for a first album it only took us a week just to do the music. Everything was basically done in a first or second take.

Any solos that stand out for you?
I don't know. I like all the songs and I like all the solos. I guess it takes someone from the outside to pick which one they like best. I really like the solo in "I'm the One," the boogie. That one was pretty much spontaneous—whereas "Runnin' with the Devil" and "On Fire" and some of the other ones were set solos. But "I'm the One" gave me a chance to space off a little bit and noodle around. Which I do a lot live; we all get crazy live. I mean, nobody spaces off to the point where it falls apart; we just add a little bit visually and sound-wise but keep it interesting.

Are there certain scales and things that you work from in putting together your solos?
Truth is I don't really know what scales they are. [*laughs*] I really don't. I know music theory and I know how to write music on paper and how to read for piano, but on guitar it's a different story. I don't know nothin' about what a scale is; I know basic notes. I can play what sounds good—what I think is good, anyway.

I hear a Ritchie Blackmore influence in your playing.

Do you use any special tunings?
Sometimes I bring the low E down to a D for some acoustic stuff; it sounds real deep.

What about picks?
Fender mediums. What I used to do was use a metal pick. A friend of mine worked in a machine shop and he always used to make me metal picks. And they were really cool—but hard to hold onto when you start sweating. They'd fly out of my hand and I'd be bummed out.

Can you talk about how you developed that fast, fluttering pick attack?
Just practice, I guess. I've been playing eight to 10 years; that's quite a while. I kind of pick at a downward angle. And I started early, which is good. A lot of people start late and play for 10 years and they don't get quite as far. I enjoy playing—that's the main thing. It's not like I was forcing myself. I wanted to be a rock and roll star. I started

FIN COSTELLO/REDFERNS/GETTY IMAGES

Since the last five or six years, I really haven't been into any one guitarist—I like everybody. I've listened to Blackmore and Jeff Beck—especially Beck's *Wired*, I like some of that stuff. Before that I just never really got into him. I didn't like him with Beck, Bogert & Appice. But the main guitarist I'd say that influenced me to play the most was Eric Clapton. I used to love the way he played—he was real smooth and had a lot of feeling. Every review I ever read of our album or my playing it's always about the Blackmore, Beck and Page influence. But I never really sat down and copped their licks like I did Clapton. I guess a lot of people think I sound like Beck or Blackmore because I do use the bar and they do also, so it kinda gets the same sound. The only thing Blackmore got me hooked on was the whammy bar. Because I never really liked the way he played that weird staccato stuff. But I feel a lot of my licks are different than theirs. Like the wide stretch things I do I try and make it sound a little bit different.

You do that one thing during "Eruption" where you're hitting a note and...

Right, right—it's like having a sixth finger on your left hand. Instead of picking you're hitting a note on the fretboard.

Was this a technique that you developed or was it just something you stumbled across?

I really don't know how to explain that. I was just sitting in my room at home, drinkin' a beer, and I remembered seeing people stretching one note and hitting the note once. They popped the finger on there to hit one note. I said, "Well, nobody is really capitalizing on that. Nobody was really doing more than just one stretch and one note real quick." So I started dickin' around and said, "Fuck! This is another technique that nobody really does!" Which it is. I haven't really seen anyone get into that as far as they could because it is a totally different sound. A lot of people listen to that and they don't even think it's a guitar. "Is that a synthesizer? A piano? What is that?"

The way you hit harmonics at the beginning of some of the songs from the album also sound different than the way other guitarists hit them.

I just liked the sound of it and I just kept workin' at it until I got the notes I wanted. You can almost do a complete scale with all the harmonics. Just gotta know where to him 'em. I guess I could be funny and say I take a lot of pills, but that ain't true.

Did you have any idea that the band would have such success? You're out touring with Montrose and Journey and you're going to Japan in March. That must feel amazing.

We're all trippin' on that it happened quick. We've been together for four years as a band. I talk to these guys in Journey and they go, "Wow, man, you guys are lucky because it happened so quick for you." But what they don't understand is we'd been together for four years before the album got out.

How were you able to promote Van Halen in the early days?

A lot of bands make a demo tape; we did that also. We went to New York with Gene Simmons from Kiss around two years ago. He saw us in a club and asked us, "Are you guys on a label or anything? Do you have a manager?" and we said, "No." So he said, "Wow, you guys are a hot band, I'd like to work with you guys." And we're going, "What do you mean?" And what it boiled down to was he wanted to take a shot at producing a rock band so we said "Sure," because he was payin' for it all. We didn't have any money and I guess basically that's why we did the tape. But then again we went to New York, made the world's most expensive demo tape, and never ended up using it. On top of not having a tape, we didn't know where in the hell to take it; we didn't know anyone.

Bands usually just take it to a record company where some clown

London, May 27, 1978.

FIN COSTELLO/REDFERNS/GETTY IMAGES

JOHN LIVZEY/REDFERNS/GETTY IMAGES

weren't a Hollywood band. Where we're from in Pasadena is really not like Hollywood at all. Anyway, it really tripped me out because when we were playin' and Mo Ostin and Ted Templeman walked in, we really didn't know. Somebody just said, "There's somebody real important out there, so play good." It was just a rainy Monday night, and there was hardly anyone in the crowd. And still Mo and Ted came backstage and said they loved it. They said, "If you don't negotiate with anyone else, you've got what you want right here." We were happy—we tripped out. Warner Bros., man, that was always the company I wanted to be with. On top of that, we got Ted Templeman to produce the record.

I talked to a lot of people who we've played with and they say, "Wow, man, we're trying to get Ted Templeman to produce our record." He's in demand and here we are, we get picked up by him.

Have you written any songs for the next album?

Oh, yeah, we write all the time. That's a good thing about the band—everybody contributes. I'm the guitarist, so I write all the riffs and shit but Dave [*Lee Roth*] writes lyrics and Al and Mike [*Anthony*] really help arrange; every song is a group effort. There's not one song that one person wrote totally.

Who's idea was it to release "You Really Got Me" as the first single?

It was a joint effort between us and Ted. The night he saw us play we played that song and he got off on it. He's going, "Hey, man, that might be a good song to put on the record." We've all been waiting to do that song anyways since we were four years old. I mean, it sounds different than the original—it's kind of updated. Van Halen–ized like a jet plane.

How has the record been selling?

Pretty good—we've sold about 350,000. We're like 29 with a bullet next week in *Billboard*. So we're kickin' some ass. When we started out with Journey and Montrose, we were brand new; I think our album was only out a week at the start of the tour. And now we're almost passing up Journey on the charts and stuff. So they're freakin'out. I think they might be happy to get rid of us. We're very energetic and we get up there and blaze on the people for 30 minutes—that's all

All we're tryin' to do is put some excitement back into rock and roll.

sittin' on a couch and smokin' a joint listens to your tape, and nothing will ever happen that way. So what we basically did was just kept playing the L.A. area everywhere. We used to put on our own shows in our hometown and draw like 3,000 people on a $4 ticket. This was way before Warner Bros. So we just developed a following that way, and the word got out.

Then you had some people from Warner Bros. come down and see the band?

Finally Ted Templeman and Mo Ostin came down to the Starwood in Hollywood, which was always kind of a bad place for us because we

we're allowed to play with them. They won't let us use any effects. For my solo, "Eruption," I do that every night live and I have this old World War II bomb which is about six or seven feet tall and I put some echo boxes in it. Usually the thing blows up at the end of my solo with all the smoke bombs, but they won't let me use it. We don't get soundchecks; we don't get shit. But we're still blazin' on the people, man—we're getting a good strong encore every night.

All we're tryin' to do is put some excitement back into rock and roll. It seems like a lot of people are old enough to be our daddies and they sound like it or they act like it—they seem energy-less. It seems like they forget what rock and roll is all about. ▪

Reprinted from **Guitar World,** *April 2004*

VHI

In 1978, Van Halen burst out of the Sunset Strip and set the music world on fire with their debut album. This is the story behind the group's rise to success and the making of *Van Halen*, the record that changed guitar-oriented rock forever.

- - - - -

by Joe Bosso

THIRTY YEARS AGO, Van Halen arrived when music was in desperate need of them. Belching fire and brimstone and fighting for their right to party while the Beastie Boys were still in middle school, their timing was impeccable. When *Van Halen*, the Pasadena, California-based group's debut album, was released on February 10, 1978, there were hardly any stars in American music. The album not only made celebrities of the group's four members—it also gave new life to guitar-oriented rock and made virtuosity a criterion for any guitarist who hoped to follow in the group's footsteps.

From the start, everything about Van Halen seemed to suggest grandness of scale: Their name, which, somewhat surprisingly, singer David Lee Roth had to convince Eddie Van Halen into using in place of the more directly size-centric Mammoth (Eddie later admitted that his surname was the perfect choice: "It sounds huge, like an atomic bomb."). Their outsized stage show, perfected at backyard keggers and wet T-shirt contests, and eventually at Sunset Strip clubs like the Whisky a Go-Go and Gazzarri's.

And, of course, their energy. Van Halen had swagger, good looks and smiles—that magical show-biz triumvirate introduced and perfected by the Beatles that had somehow become lost over the years. What's more, they and their music were fun. By the early Seventies, music was beginning to feel like work: the prog-rock movement brought staggering feats of virtuosic musicianship, but the music was full of torturous 20-minute opuses about space travel and Knights of the Round Table. Van Halen seemed to understand that music could be the antidote to cynicism, that it could make you feel alive again. "I think the thing that separated me and the rest of the band from everybody else was the fact that we just loved to play," Eddie recalled. "That's the thing: you don't *work* music, you *play* music."

There was also that sound, a ground shaker that matched the audacity of the band's ambitions. It was based on booming drums and gushers of distorted guitar, jacked up by Eddie's personally modified guitars and amplifiers (the guitarist famously used Variacs to lower the line voltage of his amps, thereby reducing head-

ROSS HALFIN

room and causing the power tubes to compress and distort more). Rarely in the annals of rock did a sound serve a band so beautifully: the higher the volume, the larger the canvas, the more inspired the music making.

Most important, there was Eddie's singular approach to the guitar, honed at first by years of obsessively studying the styles of Hendrix, Beck and, in particular, Eric Clapton. Slowing down Cream records to copy the solos to songs such as "Spoonful" brought the young guitarist only so far. By his mid-teens, out of frustration and sheer force of will, he flipped the bird to convention and became a recluse, shutting himself in his bedroom for 12 hours at a time to devote himself to the instrument and the strange and wondrous noises he heard in his head. "I used to sit on the edge of my bed with a six-pack of Schlitz Malt talls," he said. "My brother [*Alex*] would go out at 7 P.M. to party and get laid, and when he'd come back at 3 A.M., I would still be sitting in the same place, playing guitar. I did that for years."

When he finally emerged from his room and hit the Hollywood stages with Van Halen (which included Alex on drums, Michael Anthony on bass and Roth), his breathtaking abilities were nearly fully formed, as was his unorthodox hammer-on-and-pull-off technique. Eddie readily admits that he wasn't the first guitarist to employ this approach, but the manner in which he brought it to the fore, with a commitment and finesse that transcended mere gimmickry, was seen as shocking, revolutionary and, above all, baffling. "I think I got the idea of tapping watching Jimmy Page do his 'Heartbreaker' solo back in 1971," he recalled. "He was doing a pull-off to an open string, and I thought, Wait a minute, open string...pull off. I can do that, but what if I use my finger as the nut and move it around? I just kind of took it and ran with it."

Still precocious enough to be considered an *enfant terrible*, Eddie Van Halen incited strong reactions and drew legions of fascinated (and no doubt envious) guitarists to his band's shows. When performing live in those early years, he played with his back to the audience. While this might have been seen as an act of supreme humility, as if some part of him rebelled against canonization, it was in fact an act of self-preservation. His brother Alex, demonstrating uncanny prescience, had warned him that other guitarists would "rob him blind" if his tricks were exposed before the band could cut a record. It was only after the release of *Van Halen* that Eddie, secure in the knowledge that his feats of fretboard wizardry had been sufficiently documented, felt comfortable playing facing a crowd.

But even before he tracked his first note in a professional recording studio, he was putting serious distance between himself and his peers—and his heroes. Many guitarists have a talent, but to be suc-

cessful it is not enough to have talent; one must have a certain *kind* of talent. Hendrix was a shape-shifter of sound in a psychedelic, blues-based idiom. Page was a master of moods, production and arrangement. Beck was flash stylist. Clapton had tone, taste and knew his way around pop composition. With Eddie Van Halen, all of the above applied. His thing was, he could do it all. And, along with David Lee Roth, he was penning songs that were tight and tuneful— the stuff that hits are made of.

Their reputation for drawing audiences was built quickly. Soon the band was opening for the likes of Santana, UFO, Nils Lofgren and Sparks. When scenester and show promoter Rodney Bingenheimer booked Van Halen into the Starwood club, Kiss' Gene Simmons caught their act and was floored. Taking the Pasadena upstarts under his leathery wing, Simmons financed the band's first professional demo tape. Basics for the songs "Runnin' with the Devil" and "House of Pain" (the latter of which would appear on the album *1984*) were cut at Village Recorder Studios in Los Angeles. Later, Simmons, who was trying to persuade the band into calling themselves Daddy Longlegs (an idea they rejected out of hand), flew the group to New York to finish recording at Electric Ladyland Studios in New York.

It was there that Eddie had his first exposure with the practice of overdubbing; the guitarist was anything but comfortable with the process. "I tried to do it, but I just didn't know how," he said. "You have to play to yourself. I was like, 'How the hell do I do this?' I hadn't even played with another guitarist.' While in New York, Simmons arranged for the band to perform a showcase for Kiss' manager Bill Aucoin. Aucoin agreed with Simmons that Van Halen had spirit, but he felt their commercial prospects were limited; instead, the manager set his sights on signing a band called Piper, whose commercial prospects proved to be even less than limited. With their demo tape in hand, Van Halen headed back to California, buoyed by their brush with success but uncertain when their real break would come.

Although they were stars on the Sunset Strip, the band wasn't seeing much money; some gigs paid no more than $75. "Not even enough to buy equipment," Eddie recalled. "Alex and I used to go around and paint house numbers on curbs to make extra money." All of that changed during another Starwood performance when the band was introduced to Marshall Berle, nephew of comedian and TV icon Milton Berle, who became the group's manager. Berle had a flair for hype, but something about the way he talked up Van Halen and their ability to draw crowds led Warner Bros. head Mo Ostin to believe that maybe this was more than just talk—perhaps there was something to this band from Pasadena after all. And so, on a night

A new movement was taking place

and Van Halen, with a bratty authority and a rapacious sense of purpose not heard since the debut of Led Zeppelin, were leading the charge.

FIN COSTELLO/REDFERNS/GETTY IMAGES

FIN COSTELLO/REDFERNS/GETTY IMAGES

that saw heavy rain flood the Hollywood streets, Van Halen played to a nearly empty Starwood. Mo Ostin was there, along with Warner Bros. in-house producer Ted Templeman. Despite the nonexistent crowd, Van Halen played with unbridled brio. Ostin and Templeman looked at each other and smiled: They would sign the band, as in right away. "It was right out of the movies," Eddie said. "Just like that, we finally had a record deal."

Templeman, who had produced albums for Van Morrison, Carly Simon and Captain Beefheart, among others, and who enjoyed a long and fruitful association with the Doobie Brothers, was astounded by Van Halen's surfeit of strong material, and he wasted little time in hustling them into Sunset Sound Studios. Once in the studio, even less time was wasted: In only 18 days, the band raced through their entire repertoire, 40 songs in all, originals as well as covers such as the Kinks' "You Really Got Me" and John Brim's blues standard "Ice Cream Man." On the songs that didn't require a vibrato bar ("You Really Got Me," "Runnin' with the Devil," the rhythm track for "Jamie's Cryin' "), Eddie employed his main live guitar, an Ibanez "Shark" Destroyer. On other songs, he used a black-and-white striped Strat that he outfitted with a Gibson Fifties PAF humbucker.

Much to Eddie's relief, Templeman wasn't the punctilious sort; the producer was in thrall of the band's live performance qualities and insisted on keeping instrumental overdubs to a minimum. "It was a party," Eddie said of the sessions. "We played the way we

played onstage, and it was great. It didn't feel like we were making a record. We just went in, poured back a few beers and played."

The tracks for the album had almost all been cut when, one day, Templeman walked into the studio and heard Eddie and Alex warming up for a show the band was to play that night at the Whisky. According to Eddie, the two were just "dickin' around," but Templeman sensed something else was happening, a breakthrough of some sort. He watched and listened in hypnotic excitement as the guitarist's fingers danced along the fretboard. These weren't the normal scales and patterns Eddie had traditionally practiced to limber up; these were strange and exciting song fragments, a voluptuous feast of ideas, operatic in scope but performed with a savage, erotic force. Templeman had already been telling friends and associates about this marvelous new guitarist he'd been working with, going so far as to compare him to the likes of Django Reinhardt and Andrés Segovia, but now he was convinced of Eddie Van Halen's genius. He asked Eddie what it was he was playing. "Oh, that's a little solo thing I do live," he responded. Templeman didn't recall Van Halen playing it at the Starwood show he attended, but he insisted that the instrumental be fleshed out and cut for the album.

In one breathless take, after a short, bombastic intro with Alex and Michael Anthony, Eddie released an unbroken ribbon of scales, bends, dive bombs and hammer-on classical-sounding arpeggios. As he did in all of the band's songs, Eddie tuned down

From the moment people dropped the needle on *Van Halen*, they were in a state of shock.

a half step (this was done both to accommodate Roth's vocal style and to give the guitar sound more teeth). The only effects that were used were an MXR Phase 90 and a Univox EC-80 echo box (the latter of which was housed in an old WWII bomb shell that Eddie found in a junkyard). One minute and forty-two seconds after the tape started rolling, Eddie pulled his vibrato bar up after a long, descending growl and "Eruption," as it was now called, was complete. Templeman and the band were elated, but Eddie was chastened. "I didn't even play it right," he later remarked. "There's a mistake at the top end of it. To this day, whenever I hear it I always think, Man, I could've played it better."

Eddie would soon make one more screw up, only this wouldn't go down so well. With the album still months away from release, he went to the Rainbow Bar & Grill and hung out with members of a fellow Sunset Strip band called Angel. As alcohol flowed, drummer Barry Brandt began to brag about the forthcoming Angel record. Eddie, flush with pride over the album he had just cut, responded in kind. When the party moved to Brandt's house, Eddie, hell bent on blowing everybody's mind, put on a tape of *Van Halen*—and jaws were dropped. Eddie thought nothing of it—for weeks he had been playing the tape for his friends—but when he got a call from a furious Ted Templeman, informing him that Angel were in a studio frantically recording their own version of "You Really Got Me" with the intention of beating Van Halen to the punch, he realized the magnitude of his mistake. As a consequence, Warner Bros. had no choice but to rush-release Van Halen's version of the song. (It

should be noted that Angel would soon join Piper in the Oblivion bins at record shops.)

There were no riots in the streets, nobody threw anything (except guitars out of windows), but it's safe to say that from the moment people dropped the needle on *Van Halen* and heard what seemed to some sort of air-raid alarm (actually, it was the band members' car horns synced together and slowed down to ominous effect) they were in a state of shock. A new movement was taking place, and Van Halen, with a bratty authority and a rapacious sense of purpose not heard since the debut of Led Zeppelin, were leading the charge. A nearly flawless piece of pop art, *Van Halen* is one of those great rarities in music, at once simple and sophisticated, distilling the band's prodigious chops and party-hearty aesthetic into hummable melodies that took hold of one's senses and didn't let go. "Ain't Talkin' 'Bout Love," "Jamie's Cryin,' " "Runnin with the Devil," "I'm on Fire"—there isn't a bum track to be found. As both singer and carnival barker of sorts, David Lee Roth made all the right noises: surprised whoops, leering come-ons, testicle-gripping screams, hollers of "whoa now" and the like—the full panoply of orchestrated let-me-entertain-you shtick. Alex Van Halen and Michael Anthony more than held up their respective ends, providing a prizefighter's punch and, in the case of Anthony, background vocals that sailed in the air and served as the perfect counterpoint to Roth's gruff voice.

Of course, there was Eddie. Of all the young guitarists who ever issued a debut record, he's the one who delivered on promises he never had to make. Dispensing with the usual wobbly preamble of a flawed but ambitious first record, he burst through the gate as a musician who valued substance and emotional contact over mere technical flash. With poetry in his heart and a panoramic vision of where he was headed, he never had to develop into something special, for he was already there. Being thrust into the pantheon of greats at such a tender age (he was 22 at the time) and so early in his career can be ruinous to most musicians, but Eddie's extraordinary energy and thirst for innovation proved to be invaluable strengths. Guitarists the world over saw the rashness and speed of his gifts and emulated him in a way that no musician has ever had to endure. "Eruption" was and continues to be a litmus test for budding ax slingers—what Frank Zappa's "The Black Page" is to drummers, so, too, Eddie's tour de force is to guitarists. But it's also a cul-de-sac, for no matter how hard everyone tried to catch up to Eddie Van Halen, he was burning up the ground as fast as he could run.

Thirty-two years on, it continues unabated. ◪

FRANK WHITE (RIGHT)

BOTTOMS UP!

Their 1979 New Year's Eve gig may have been canceled due to David Lee Roth's broken foot, but that didn't keep Van Halen from partying it up during the recording of *Van Halen II.*

- - - - -

by Steven Rosen

PAGE 047

When did you start working on the second album?
We started on the Monday after our last gig—we jumped in right away because we figured we might as well get it out of the way. That was about two weeks ago. We were obviously a lot tighter than if we took a couple weeks off and partied it up every weekend. So Ted [*Templeman, producer*] suggested it and we said, "Yeah, we were gonna ask you if we could do it right away." We were much tighter because we'd just played for 10 straight months. Even if you're half asleep there's something there—you're just tight without knowing it. We went in Monday and Tuesday we rehearsed—Wednesday and Thursday we recorded about four or five songs. And then we took off because we had to write some more songs.

You didn't have the album already written?
No, not at all actually.

Did you think the first album would have done as well as it did?
Hell no! Who knows? The next one might bomb. [*laughs*] I feel pretty good about this one; the first one I had no idea. Even though we took

the same approach on this one. We just do what we come up with as opposed to forcing ourselves to write something commercial. Some of the stuff will probably never get any airplay. But that's what I really like—I get off on playing that stuff. I like the hard stuff.

Did you take what you learned on the first album and apply it to this one?
It was actually exactly like the first record—we just set up in a big room. I used almost everything I used onstage, only I used my old Marshalls as opposed to brand new ones that I use onstage. I don't like using the old ones onstage because I've lost 'em before and they sound, to my ear, so good. I put them in a closet and leave them there.

So there wasn't much overdubbing this time either?
Oh, not at all. There will be 10 songs on the album and three of them have guitar overdubs. The rest are live.

What's the album called?
Van Halen...

FIN COSTELLO/REDFERNS/GETTY IMAGES (PREVIOUS SPREAD); NEIL ZLOZOWER/ATLASICONS.COM (THIS PAGE)

all sequenced, I bet it won't be at all like the first one.

How would you describe the sound of the album?
It's just much fuller. Also Ted and Donn Landee, the engineer, for the first record they weren't quite sure of what we wanted and they weren't too familiar with our sound and now they are. So I guess it's just growing. We play better, we write better, and they in turn know how to bring the sound out better for us. Ted said when we rehearsed, "God, I can't believe how tight you guys are compared to the first record."

Can you give me a rundown of the songs?
I can't even remember the songs. I can go out and get the tape. [*Edward runs outside and retrieves the cassette from his car stereo.*] Okay, the first song on the tape is "Outta Love Again," which sounds like [*Tower of Power's*] "What Is Hip." It sounds more funky. Everyone can relate to that; everyone falls in love and out of love. I really like that song because it makes the drums shine. That kinda pissed me off about the first record—that there wasn't enough drums. On this album there's a lot more spots where the bass and drums are spotlighted as opposed to the guitar. And "Outta Love Again" is one of the songs where I think the drumming is real good.

The next song is "Somebody Get Me a Doctor."
That was one written around the same time as "Runnin' with the Devil." It was an old favorite of ours and people who used to follow us around before we ever had a record out. Basically what we do in the studio is we sit with Ted and we pick out which songs we want to do. One out of the four of us might say, "Hey, let's do this one" and the other guys will go, "Nah, why don't we try this one?" So "Somebody Get Me a Doctor" didn't make the first record. It's about being high and feeling good and ODing and stuff like that.

The next one is "Women in Love" and that's a trippy one. If you follow the lyrics you can look at it two ways: It's like a guy who is going out with a chick and as opposed to the conventional way of losing a chick to a guy, he loses his chick 'cause his chick runs off with another chick. You know—women in love!

What is happening at the beginning of the song?
There are harmonics in the intro and it sounds different. It kinda sounds like I used a harmonizer but I didn't; all I did was double it. It sounds real neat. I used a regular Strat on that; I put it together myself. I have a Telly pickup in the back, a Fat Strat and something else. And I just had a junk body lying around and I threw it together in like a day and I had a Danelectro neck that I put on it. I only used it for one part; a quiet little intro. Because that other guitar is too ballsy sounding to play quiet and clean. That's about it for that one.

You did a cover song on this album?
"You're No Good," which doesn't sound at all like the original. I've never actually heard the original. Linda Ronstadt didn't write the song. [*The song was written by Clint Ballard, Jr.—Ed.*] It's a great song, I think. We used to do that song when we played Gazzarri's, only we did it like the original record; we didn't do it our own way. When we were in the studio to record it I couldn't even remember how it went. I just started noodling around and that's how it came about. We never even listened to the record. I just remembered the changes and because I didn't listen to the record, it didn't sound the same. I just kinda thought back about the basics of the song and that's how it ended up. At least this way we'll be able to pull it off live.

Being able to play a song live is a consideration in not doing a lot of overdubs?
Sure. That's the main reason we don't do a lot of overdubs. Like if

...Two?
Yeah. I didn't say it, you said it. No, it's just gonna have the logo on the front and on top where it says Van Halen it'll say *Van Halen II* just so the audience will know it's not the first one—it's the second one. But we don't mean to bill it as *Van Halen II* or like *Queen II*.

You didn't consciously try to write the types of songs that were on the first album? You didn't write another "Runnin' with the Devil"?
No. The songs aren't at all the same. Well, the first album too we didn't consciously write "Devil." It just came out that way. It wasn't like, "Hey, we need a song with the bass going *bomp bomp bomp* [*mimics opening lick*]. It's just the way it happened. I'm real happy with this record because it still sounds like Van Halen, which is three instruments and voices with very few overdubs and very live sounding. As opposed to other bands—without mentioning any names—who do try and re-do their first album. They think, Oh, wow, we hit it with that one and we've got to follow the same format. Which we didn't do at all. When the record comes out and it's

Recording *Women and Children First* at Sunset Sound in Hollywood, 1979.

NEIL ZLOZOWER/ATLASICONS.COM

Sometimes you start thinking so much that you blow it.

I do something that's the main part of the song as an overdub and I can't do it live, people are gonna miss it. They'll say, "Hey, it doesn't sound the same." So when we do overdubs, they're real subtle little things that just enhance the sound as opposed to being a real melodic main thing or something. We just depend on the rhythm section and guitar for solos and singing for melody.

Talk about "Bottoms Up!"
It's a proven song because in the 10 months we toured, six months of it at least we played it every night for our encore song everywhere from Texas to Japan—they loved it. There's a good solo in that one too. Personally, I hate soloing to boogies; it's such a weird beat and it doesn't really fit my style that well. I like to noodle out of the rhythm as opposed to playing in the beat, so I was pretty happy with it.

Then there's "Light Up the Sky," and that's my favorite. I wrote that song right after our first record was recorded. I used to dick around and play it for the guys and it was like, "Oh, Eddie's got a new riff," and nobody really said anything. And then when we came back off tour, we played all our new riffs and songs and whatever for Ted and he really liked that one. I was totally surprised because it was a little more progressive; the changes are a little more bent than the commercial and simple stuff. So I was happy that he liked that.

What else is on the new album?
"Beautiful Girls" is a happy one. [*plays the riff on the guitar*] The theme of that song is pretty much, "I got a drink in my hand, I got my toes in the sand/I'm feelin' good with a beautiful girl." It's a happy song to kind of balance it out. I hate some records; you listen to it and it's just happy-happy all the way through. There's a way to write a song where the music is up but it's still got a serious type of theme and we got a little bit of both on this record. Some songs that sound real happy, poppy, sing-along type of stuff and the other stuff is drinking a bottle of booze and fucking. That'll be a good one, I think—I like it on the tape. "D.O.A." is a good one too. Just being an outlaw and everybody is out to get you—dead or alive type of thing.

Then there's Mike's bass solo, which we need to call something. It's up to him. I named my solo "Eruption" because it kinda sounded like it. I don't know what Mike should call his bass solo. He might not win awards for being a great bass player but just the sound he gets out of it really makes a vibe; it sets a mood. When you hear it, you think of something as opposed to thinking, Oh, he's a good bass player. It sounds like animals or something—animals out late at night out to get you. It will probably be the intro into "You're No Good." Just like my solo was an intro to "You Really Got Me." If "You're No Good" is ever a single, I don't think it'll be on there. Just like "You Really Got Me" was a single and it didn't have the solo on it.

You must be really pleased with your playing on this album.
Definitely. There's a lot of guitar tricks on it but some of them are more subtle than the last record—they're not as obvious. Like when you heard the harmonic thing, a lot of people won't even think it's a guitar but it is. I like doing stuff like that—just tricks where people trip when they find out it's a guitar. They go, "Whoa!" I read a review once of our

first album and they didn't even think the finger thing that I did for "Eruption" was a guitar. They just bypassed it and said, "Oh, a synthesizer solo by Edward Van Halen." I just tripped out; if this guy took the time to find out what I was doing he'd know it was a guitar.

Have you thought about maybe adding keyboards to the sound of the band?
When we recorded the first album, I had no idea what this next one would be like. To me it's a logical progression but it still sounds like Van Halen. There have been bands who put out one record and the next one sounds too different. Have you ever heard of a band called Stray Dog? Their first album is great and the second one sounds so different.

Are there any acoustics on the album?
Yeah. There's one song that we still might do, an acoustic song called "Angel Eyes." It's a real neat song. Dave wrote the melody and chord changes. He plays acoustic somewhat; he used to do solo stuff before. That's where "Ice Cream Man" came from; he used to play that acoustic at the Ice House [*club in Pasadena*] all the time. We just said, "Hey, why don't you do that and we'll just come in halfway through?" And "Angel Eyes," I think the reason we might not put it on is because it's too much of a change. It's a total acoustic song and I think people might look at it like, "Oh, they had to stick one on there just for the hell of putting it on." So we probably won't because if we did put it on that ain't why we'd do it—it's just a good song. So maybe later on when we are doing different things, it'll fit better.

What you played for me sounded pretty ballsy.
This album, to me, sounds heavier than the first—the overall sound is just so much fuller. The songs might not be based on riffs as much as the first, but in my mind I still consider it harder sounding. But smoother too...I don't know how to explain it.

So how did Dave break his foot?
Oh, yeah, let me tell you about that. The picture on the back of the cover is the shot where he broke his foot. It is a trippy picture when you see it. He's way up in the air with his feet out and with the mic and the funny thing is he's still holding onto the mic stand. He's wearing Capezio dance shoes which are no good if you're bouncing up and down on cement. He really wrecked up his foot. And then on the inside Dave is sitting there with a cane and a cast on his foot.

Have you made a lot of money so far?
I don't know yet; we've got to meet with our accountants next week to see what we've made. It sounds funny, man, but I still feel like a kid; it still hasn't fazed me. Even if I made a lot of money, I don't know what the fuck to do with it. I went out and bought myself a $700 car. What the fuck? I still live at home. The first thing I'm going to do is get my dad to retire. Even just weekly checks out of our corporation we're making more than he is a week. So Al and I said, "Quit your job." He's been working seven days a week ever since we came to this country and we're gonna buy him a boat and retire him so he can go fishing. ◼

BOB LEAFE/FRANK WHITE PHOTO AGENCY

THIRD POWER

Shortly before the March 1980 release of Van Halen's third record, *Women and Children First*, Eddie Van Halen sat with writer Steven Rosen to discuss the band's most varied album to date.

– – – – –

by Steven Rosen

What has the process been like for this third album?
It's hard for me to tell you. It seems like it's taken so long but it's all been the red tape stuff. We did all the music, the actual recording, in four days except for the acoustic song; we did that at the very end. And then the week after that we sang for four days.

There are a lot of new textures on the record, like electric piano.
Yeah, I play piano on "And the Cradle Will Rock…" We were doing a bus tour last year and we said, "Well, what are we gonna do different on the next record?" So I said, "What the hell?" I'll go out and buy a little Wurlitzer and plink on it and that's how I came up with the music for that. That was first take by the way, except for the guitar overdubs, which I did later because I can't play piano and guitar at the same time. And no one else in the band can play guitar.

How will you pull that off live?
Mike's [*Anthony, bass*] gonna play it [*electric piano*]. My brother [*Alex*] said, "Don't play piano. Don't be a Sammy Davis, Jr., a jack-of-all-trades and master of none. Just stick to guitar." So Mike is gonna play key bass like the Doors used to use, one of those Rhodes key bass things and a Wurlitzer piano. We all pretty much play keyboards but I did write the song and play it on the record.
Let me tell you about the piano song because that's a rather unusual sound for a piano. I blazed it through my little pedal board and my Marshalls and the noise that you hear in the beginning is just an MXR flanger and banging on the lower register of the piano. In doing that, I busted one of the keys on my piano. But for better or worse, it came out on the record.

What is the song about?
It's about a kid you might say who is deprived of rock and roll but the cradle will rock—no matter what happens to him he's still gonna rock.

Like the first two records, there aren't many overdubs on this one?
I overdubbed the solo on "And the Cradle Will Rock…" and the solo is overdubbed on "Everybody Wants Some!!" because it's melodic. I prefer to overdub set melodic solos. Like on the first album I would do the solo and overdub the rhythm track. If it was a melodic solo, I would play the solo on the basic track and then overdub a rhythm. But this time Ted [*Templeman, producer*]

thought it would flow better if I just played rhythm all the way through. And the very end of "Fools" I overdubbed a basic guitar. But that's it, so there's actually three overdubs on guitar. Oh, and on "Simple Rhyme" I overdubbed the 12-string.

Had you played much 12-string before this?
No, it was a hassle and a half tuning the damn thing, though. I swear to God, man, we got this funky SIR Rickenbacker job with six-month old rusted strings on it and shit.

It almost sounds like an acoustic 12-string.
I just played it real quiet. I played it direct and miked it so it sounds like an acoustic guitar, but it still has kind of an electric sound to it.

Tell me about some of the other songs.
"And the Cradle Will Rock…" was brand new, "Everybody Wants Some!!" and "Romeo Delight" were brand new, and "Could This Be Magic?" was brand new and the intro and shit. "Loss of Control" we reworked so it wouldn't sound as punk. I wrote it at the same time I wrote "Ain't Talkin' 'Bout Love." "Whiskey" [*Take Your Whiskey Home*] was an old song and we decided to change that a bit with the acoustic intro. Everything else is new; there are only two songs on here that were worked out before we went into the studio. "Could This Be Magic?" is the acoustic song where we sound like a bunch of drunk fool sailors just getting into town. Actually the hook of the album title is in that: "Better save the women and children first." But it's not the title track.

What is the title of the album?
Women and Children First, but we decided to call the song "Could This Be Magic?" so all the radio program directors wouldn't play that song first if we called it "Women and Children First."

There's some slide in "Could This Be Magic?"
The first time I ever played slide. We were a little bit drunk and the guys go, "Doesn't sound right, Ed, why don't you try playing slide?" I'm going, "Uh oh, I've never played slide, guys." They're going, "Just fake it." I just played it regular guitar tuning; I didn't re-tune. A lot of people tune especially for slide; I don't even know how to tune it that way. I just played it normal.

There are a lot of these little intro bits that musically stand on their own and really have nothing to do with the songs that follow.
Yeah. "Tora! Tora!" is the introduction to "Loss of Control," which is kind of appropriately titled. It sounds like a Spitfire taking off or something.

How did you do that intro?
I did it with one of those Floyd Rose vibrato bar things.

When we were listening to the tape, you pointed out these little phrases that were actually wrong notes and stuff. But you left them in.
Sometimes I do shit on a record, man, and it's just a freak little thing. I love mistakes because you can never re-do them exactly the same; you never can. They're just freak things. And a lot of times some good shit comes out.

"Fools" has a little mistake in it?

Yeah, I don't even know how I did it; it was really a freak thing. It sounds weird; it sounds like I'm slipping. It's just one of those things where you say, "Wait a minute...what is that?" I wasn't sure whether I liked it or not but then since I couldn't exactly figure out how I did, I said, "Yeah, I like it."

No solo songs like "Eruption" or "Spanish Fly"?

No, I did a small introduction to "Fools," which is a little guitar freakout for a couple seconds. That should fulfill the guitar freaks.

Your homemade Strat is still the main guitar?

Yeah, it's the only one I used. Oh, wait, I used a 335 for the solo in "And the Cradle Will Rock..." For some reason when I play a 335, I can really blaze fast. It's just a different feel for a guitar.

What about live?

Yeah. I just had Linn Ellsworth make me a Strat body; it's as thick as a Les Paul. Real fat, made out of mahogany and I'm in the process of painting it. It's real heavy but it gets a lot of tone. Using the Floyd Rose tremolo thing which I like and I don't like—it has its advantages and disadvantages—I have gotten used to using it live. So that's pretty much what I do use live. I have it on one guitar so far; it'll be on the new one. For some reason, the metal his tremolo is made out of is real brittle sounding. And I've tried everything to get a tone out of the damn thing and I couldn't. I had it on one guitar and I just couldn't get a sound out of it. So I had Linn Ellsworth make me a body twice as thick hoping that would make up for the brittleness of the metal.

You like the original Fender Strat tailpieces?

I prefer the old tailpieces. For some reason they get a lot more tone than all this other garbage. Mighty Mite brass stuff. Brass? I don't know, man, it just doesn't seem to work for me. I can't get a tone out of it. For some reason the old stuff is just the best. It manages to get the sound I like.

Is the whammy bar still a big part of what you do?

I didn't freak out on the bar as much as I usually do. Just so it would sound a little different.

When you go back out on the road, will you be doing a bunch of these new songs?

Yeah, it's actually very difficult for us to figure out what to play now. We have three albums to choose from. It would seem easy to pick but actually it's harder to pick because we don't know which ones to do. Looking at it now with three albums' worth of material that we can play, I go, "God, I don't see how we pulled it off our first year with only eight songs to play." I'm sure we'll do more than half of this new album.

Which songs will you do?

I know we'll do "And the Cradle Will Rock...," "Everybody Wants Some!!" "Romeo Delight," "Loss of Control" and "Simple Rhyme." And we're debating on whether we're gonna do "Could This Be Magic?" which is the acoustic song. I think we might do that instead of "Ice Cream Man" because it's nice to have an acoustic song in the set.

Do you pick the bands that open for you on tour?

Actually the bands that we pick won't play with us. Nobody will play with us. It's hard. Come one, come all—we're not afraid of anybody. They're afraid. Last year every band that played with us got booted off somewhere along the line. Seriously it really freaked me out. Our first show last year was in Fresno and the Fabulous Poodles opened up and got booed off the stage. We don't want to pull a Zeppelin and just play two and a half hours by ourselves, because kids get tired of that.

Didn't you also have a problem with Rick Derringer?

Yeah, I don't want to talk about that.

I had interviewed Rick a while ago and he was talking about guitar players and I said, "Who do you listen to?" and he said, "I listen to everybody. Eddie Van Halen is fantastic."

He just acted like an asshole when I talked to him. For him to play like me or cop my style is fine. But to play my solo almost note-for-note and then go into our ending song, that's a little different. He's a nice guy and I had asked him, "Don't do exactly what we do," because that would be just like us playing it twice.

So are you happy with the album?

Yeah, I love it. I think it's our best one yet because it's got more variety. It's not too guitar dominated; it's just got a little bit of everything on it. It's got acoustic, it's got piano, it's got the ball-bustin' rock. It's got it all.

Don't you think people listen to Van Halen specifically to hear your guitar playing and to see what new sounds you've created?

I'm sure they listen to it for the overall thing. I don't think they listen to it just for my playing. But I think there's enough of my playing on there to satisfy them.

Have you ever thought about what people have come to expect from you as a guitar player? Is there pressure to keep constantly coming up with new stuff on the guitar?

It seems like it would but it doesn't. 'Cause the way I've gotten to where I've gotten is just by doing what I do without worrying about, "Oh, I gotta do this. I gotta make sure I get better." I don't really think I get better. I just change. You can only get so fast, you can only twang so much. It's a matter of change more, I think, than getting better. I think it's changed from the first album to the second and from the second to the third. I don't want to call it maturing or anything. If you're exposed to different things you tend to play different now and then. And right now I'm playing a little different than I have in the last couple of years. It still sounds like me. I still think you'll be able to pick up on the sound and the style right away but I'm using a different combination of notes now and then. Playing different licks and different riffs and different little noises. There's noises on this record that people probably wouldn't even know what it is. Sure, there are certain licks that I do consciously and the best ones usually come out when I'm not thinking.

Do you hear other people playing like Eddie Van Halen?

I'm not trying to sound egotistical but they try to. And I actually think it's better that they try to because it comes off as a little different. Whereas if they play exactly like me it's gonna sound like me. Just like when I grew up playing, I tried playing exactly like some people but I just couldn't. I think that's how my style developed. Out of the mere fact that I couldn't play like someone else. I had to do something, I had to come up with something myself.

Is there any new music that you like?

I love Allan Holdsworth. I'm into the last album he did with Bruford. It still amazes me every time I hear it. That fucker is good. U.K. opened for us once in Reno and I couldn't believe it. I shit my pants. They're going, "U.K. is opening for you." I said, "Okay, groovy." I never heard of U.K. And then all of a sudden I looked at Al and said, "Isn't that Bill Bruford?" These guys were fucking playing but the people weren't very receptive to them at all. Goddamn that dude is really a strange player. It sounds like he doesn't pick a lot, that's why it sounds so smooth. You can never hear the attack of his pick. I'd love to hear him play with [*Tim*] Bogert. If I ever played bass, that's how I'd want to play. Put it that way. That's what I don't understand—that he's not that respected or that famous for being that good. It's almost like Holdsworth. He's

I don't really think I get better.
I just change.

so fucking good but he doesn't get the credit.

What about people like Ted Nugent and Ace Frehley?
Ted is a nice guy but I don't really like the way he plays too much. He looks at it like Gene Simmons. Gene is a real nice guy; he always writes us. He wanted me and Al to play on his solo album but we couldn't because we were on tour. A couple songs on the record we played on the demo tape and they sounded much better. They sounded real good; I liked 'em. "Tunnel of Love," but it's done different; it's half-beat on this one but it was more rock when me and Al played it. And the other one was "Christine Sixteen." Remember the solo in that? I wrote the solo for that and it sounded so good when we played with him because I double-tracked it. It was a double solo, a double lead. It sounded so good and then all of a sudden their record comes out [Love Gun] and they played the same solo but it sounded like he used some kind of octave box. It didn't sound the same. "That guy, he fucked up my solo." It sounded good; it was a good melodic little thing that really fit in.

I was surprised with Ace Frehley's solo album. I liked it. It's just more "up." At least he stepped out a little bit. I mean, he's not that great of a guitarist either. The way he plays sounds so uncoordinated. I don't want to sit here and cut all these people down. I always still look at myself like a kid looking at these guys like they're big. I don't know, I just don't look at myself equal to them. So I find myself cutting them down, but I don't really mean to. Sometimes these guys just play with a weird kind of vibrato and they always seem to miss the note. They go everywhere around it [*picks up a guitar and mimics a very bad guitar player with a lifeless finger vibrato*].

Ted Templeman and Donn Landee obviously worked on this one.
Oh, yeah, did a great job, I think. Excellent job.

They must be used to the Van Halen system of madness by now.
Yeah, I think it's a breath of fresh air for them. Everything else they do is very middle of the road to mellow. We are the only rock thing that they produce. Even out of rock bands, I think we lean to the extreme. ◼

NEIL ZLOZOWER/ATLASICONS.COM

SO THIS IS LOVE

As Van Halen's 1982 album *Diver Down* raced up the charts, Eddie Van Halen looked back with great fondness on that album's monumental predecessor, 1981's *Fair Warning*.

- - - - -

by Steven Rosen

N MANY WAYS, *Fair Warning* was the least understood of all the Van Halen albums. Today, veiled rumblings still echo about the record's latent darkness, the lack of a big single and the unorthodox sound and style of many of its tracks. Yet for those willing to see past all of that and wade into the rivers of guitars so intelligently orchestrated, what awaited them was a baffling array of six-string motifs, intersecting walls of rhythm, and solos gloriously and passionately executed. Everyone knows about the invention and imagination on *Van Halen* and the keyboards and charisma of *1984*. But sandwiched between the two is an oft-times overlooked miracle of electric guitar, a savage and compelling vision from the most important instrumentalist to emerge in the last two and a half decades.

This conversation took place in 1982 immediately following the release of *Diver Down*. Obviously Edward addressed the newest album but felt that in order to put it more in perspective, it was necessary to look back at the one that came before. Hunkered down in the living room of his Coldwater Canyon home, frosty beers and mixed drinks flowing nicely, he revisited *Fair Warning* to reveal the secrets and sacrifices surrounding that record's genesis. Clutching an unplugged electric guitar for ballast, Van Halen punctuated his responses by playing the various riffs being discussed. Even acousti-cally, these bits and pieces sounded as big as heaven crashing.

Fair Warning was different than the earlier albums. On the first three records you tended to minimize overdubs while on this one you seemed to focus on multiple guitar parts.
Oh, yeah, I think the most ever. I did a lot of overdubbing and it came out real good, I think. It was a very different approach from my standpoint, and I'm very happy with it—and I love the solos that I did. I'm not in the slightest way unhappy with any solo I did on that record; I like 'em all.

Was this a technique you specifically wanted to try? Or did the songs demand this sort of elaborate treatment?
I gotta say that, okay, *Fair Warning*, out of our five albums, was done, most of it, the complete opposite of *Diver Down*. Most of it was done in the studio.

The songs were worked up in the studio?
Yes; I had basic ideas. We came off tour and everyone goes, "Whadd'ya got, Eddie?" and I showed them basic ideas and we went from there. Instead of working them up before we went in the studio, we worked them out *in* the studio. And I think I'm doing some of my best solos on that record.

I don't know if this sounds egoed out but I kind of amaze myself sometimes when I look back at the tunes and the music that I've written. I think it's good; I'm going, "Goddamn." I mean, on *Fair Warning*, everything on it I came up within two weeks. I also weighed 125 pounds; I lost a lot of weight and a lot of sleep because I knew it had to be done.

I mean, like, "Sinner's Swing!" was spontaneous; that was a first take. It sounds like falling down the stairs. I like the solo in "Push Comes to Shove" too—actually, I like every solo that I did on that record. including "Unchained" and the one on "Hear About It Later"

with those little countermelodies.

Fair Warning is the most expensive album we've done so far, though. It took longer and you can blame that on me—it's my fault, but I just wanted to approach it different. I wanted to do more over-dubbing so it took time. But I like it all; it fits.

The way you start the solo in "Push Comes to Shove" with those simple hammers and that minor feel just sends shivers up your spine.
Because it was a break and everything stopped.

It just cries out with this thematic melody. In fact it sounds like it's the opening notes of a movie score.
That's the only solo ever in my life except for "Secrets" [*Diver Down*] and "Push Comes to Shove" that I semi worked out. I worked out the beginning of "Secrets" and especially the last part; I planned it. And I might have done a couple of takes of it and one was better than the other but they were all basically pretty much the same. And "Push Comes to Shove" and "Secrets" are the only two songs ever on any album that I planned.

"Push Comes to Shove" was a real different type of track for the

WARING ABBOTT/MICHAEL OCHS ARCHIVES/GETTY IMAGES (PREVIOUS SPREAD); RICHARD E. AARON/REDFERNS/GETTY IMAGES (THIS PAGE)

We do whatever we want to do and that's it.

band. Sort of a combination of the Stones, R&B, funk and reggae.
Oh, definitely; I think "Secrets" is, too.

Do you think that "Push Comes to Shove" was a sort of stepping-stone to creating "Secrets"? Not that either song vaguely resembles the other.
Yeah, I know what you mean. What I think about the band is that you cannot label us. You cannot call us heavy metal; you cannot call us progressive; you cannot call us mellow; you cannot call us whatever you want to call us. We do whatever we want to do and that's it. Take it or leave it. If you don't like it, you don't like it; if you do, you do. But we do what we want to do. Period.

Do you have any feelings about David Lee Roth's vocals on the album?
The truth is, I don't think he sang as good as I played. He took off for two weeks and again it was, "What do you got, Eddie?" and I had pretty much basic ideas for everything that is on the record. I worked my ass off on that one. But I love it; it's my life. At least Dave pulls his weight. Mike [*Anthony, bass*] doesn't. He doesn't do anything; he has no input whatsoever. Period. But he has remodeled his whole house and bought himself a Turbo Carrera off the money he's made off of us. Whatever.

How exactly do you and Dave work on a track? Do you present him with a piece of music and suggest melodies and places in the song where you hear a verse or chorus?
Here's what happens: I come up with the music. Like 99.9 percent I have every part then Alex usually hears everything I come up with before anyone else. And then sometimes Ted [*Templeman, producer*]. So the music comes first. Then melody is applied and then lyrics.

But where does that melody come from?
Depends. Dave writes 99.9 percent of the lyrics. A lot of times we don't like a word here and there and we'll change it. I'd say melody comes from Dave a lot, comes from Al [*Alex Van Halen, drums*] a lot, and I am more involved in the music than anything else.

The guitars on the album are so beautifully composed and structured that it must make it infinitely more difficult to perform them without the support of the bass.
It doesn't make it harder to play because I'll tell you the honest-to-God fucking truth—that since day one, I never liked Mike's sound and I could never hear him. I can never hear him play when we play. Period. All I have live in my monitors is Al, a little bit of Dave's vocals, a little bit of mine, a little bit of Mike's, and all I hear is myself and my brother. In the studio, it's the same.

Which brings us to another remarkable aspect of the album and that is the rhythm playing. Your sense of rhythm is so highly developed—is that how you're able to pull off these parts without hearing a bass track?
I don't know. I am absolutely a rhythmic player. I work more off of rhythm than I do...I'm not saying that I'm not melodic at all. I can be melodic if I want to be. But most of my spontaneous stuff is not melodic; it does have a certain edge to it where it goes high, low, in-between, slow, fast and whatever. But that's why I like "Push Comes to Shove," which I think is melodic, and "Secrets" is melodic and maybe even the solo on "Dancing in the Streets" or whatever.

The other night I went over to Frank Zappa's house and played him *Fair Warning* all the way through and I was listening and I was amazed. I'm going, "I did that?" Frank tripped. He was going, "I thought you guys were just another fuckin' AC/DC!" When I talked to him on the phone [*Edward spent a fair amount of time over at Zappa's house while working on music with son Dweezil—Ed.*], the first thing he said to me was, "Thank you very much for reinventing the electric guitar."

NEIL ZLOZOWER/ATLASICONS.COM

Reprinted from **Guitar World,** *July 1985*

THE LIFE AND TIMES OF VAN HALEN

As "Jump" hit *Billboard*'s Number One slot in 1984, *Guitar World* presented one of the first interviews from 5150, Edward's new home studio.

– – – – –

by Steven Rosen

EDWARD VAN HALEN, born in Nijmegen, the Netherlands, on January 26, 1957, has been disseminating what he calls "the brown sound" now for over six years, or since the Pasadena quartet released its self-titled debut album. *Van Halen* sold over two million copies, with every subsequent release—*Van Halen II, Women and Children First, Fair Warning, Diver Down* and *1984*—selling well in excess of one million units. *1984* finished sixth on *Billboard*'s Top Albums of 1984; the "Jump" single ranked sixth as well, after occupying the coveted Number One position for a time.

FIN COSTELLO/REDFERNS/GETTY IMAGES

1984 is the first album recorded at Edward's 16-track home studio, 5150 (a name derived from an L.A. police code for the criminally insane). The cohesive batch of songs on the album re-establishes the balance and atmosphere which were notably absent from the group's *Diver Down* effort. Edward also establishes himself as a formidable synthesist on such tracks as the title song, "I'll Wait" and, of course, "Jump."

Coming off yet another world tour, Edward recently set aside several days to discuss *1984*, and the music he made prior to this breakthrough sixth album. Most of the conversations took place at 5150, amidst scattered guitars, reels of two-inch tape and empty beer cans. Rarely was the studio phone silent for more than an hour during our time together; it was during the unlikely lapses that much of the following interview took place.

Edward's schedule, even by a musician's standards, is a severe one. He ordinarily works from early evening to well past noon, experimenting with new guitars, programming rhythms on his Linn-Drum and working on bits and pieces of music stashed on hundreds of scattered cassettes. "Noodling," he calls it.

Van Halen is wary of interviews—and interviewers—but quite adept at fielding questions. He is deliberate with his responses, and refreshingly forthright. As a result, what follows is a genuinely intimate look at the guitarist who, more than anyone since the golden days of the late Sixties, has redefined the limits of the electric six-string.

Eddie Van Halen's character hasn't changed. He is truly taken aback by compliments. Despite his enormous success, he is the same self-effacing man he was years ago, when the Van Halen group first signed with Warner Bros.

Here, then, is Edward Van Halen—father of the "brown sound."

1984 was a productive year for Van Halen.
The best year we've had. We started to see not just success, but also the satisfaction of knowing what we can accomplish. It was a strong year in every aspect.

Do you think it's the best music you've made?
That's hard to say. I like everything we've done.

Did you think the *1984* album would be so well-received?
I figured that it was good and would get noticed. But how can anyone say, "This is going to go Platinum"?

Are you the final arbiter of what eventually makes it on record?
I'm not the only one involved. If the rest of the guys don't like something, I'm outvoted. But with regard to my happiness about something we've recorded, what I think of it is more important. If I like it and other people don't, of course my reaction might be, "Why don't they like it?" But I don't write to please other people. It's nice, but you have to please yourself first.

You've written songs that never made their way to vinyl.
That's because Ted [*Templeman, Van Halen producer*] or somebody in the band voted against it, and decided it wasn't right for that point in time. "House of Pain" [1984] was written before we were signed. A lot of things I write aren't accepted with open arms, whether it's because of the instrumentation or that they just don't like the music.

What if you feel very strongly about a particular song?
"I'll Wait" [1984] was one. Donn [*Landee, Edward's engineer*] and I both felt very strongly about it. Nobody else did, so we put it down ourselves. Then they heard it and said [*in dumb-struck tone*], "Uh, what's that?" I'm not going to sit there and cry if they don't like it, but sometimes something gets lost in the translation of an idea.

Does that happen very often?
Obviously, it happens a lot. But the thing is, when you put it down

on tape and they still don't like it, then there isn't a whole lot of room for miscommunication.

Do you think the difference in musical tastes between you and David Lee Roth has made Van Halen what it is?
I'm sure that has had something to do with it, but it's not necessarily just Dave. It's Al and Ted and Donn and me all having different musical tastes. But it's not even musical tastes. Music is music, and if something is good and you like it, it's good. I like some jazz, I like some punk. Dave and Al listen to just about everything.

Do you bounce ideas off [*bassist*] Mike Anthony?
I show my ideas to him along with everyone else. He generally goes along with the majority and usually doesn't have any strong preferences.

How close is the final version of a song to the original demo?
Generally, there isn't much rewriting. Parts might be rearranged or chopped here and there.

Does Ted help with these arrangements?
[*pauses*] Yes and no. He has a talent that, in a way, is unbeatable. But sometimes he doesn't allow other ideas to develop before he puts his this-is-the-way-to-go thing to it. And that's not putting him down at all. You can't expect any two people to think and feel identically about an idea. But that's how ideas get totally twisted and distorted from the original seed: people get involved in how they think it should sound. And I'm sure I'm as guilty of this as Ted

NEIL ZLOZOWER/ATLASICONS.COM

NEIL ZLOZOWER/ATLASICONS.COM

and Al and Dave and everyone put together.

Where would you be if you had never gotten involved with Ted Templeman?

I think we'd be where we are. But Ted tends to look for singles, or songs that could be a single for radio play; that's his way of thinking. We think differently. Period. I think we definitely complement him and vice-versa. Both parties would be different without the other. It's hard to say whether it would be better or worse. I think the reason we sound different is that the individuals in the band have their own styles.

seems to be the yardstick by which every other rock band is measured. Do you think that's because you write great songs?

What's a great song? Lots of people think a song without singing is not a song. Tell that to Beethoven and he'll kick your ass.

Would you like to have been Beethoven?

I wouldn't want to have died at the age he did [57]. Anyone who wouldn't want to be as respected as he is would be a fool. I'm happy being who I am—I wouldn't want to be anybody else.

How would you say your songwriting has grown?

It just changes. I guess, if I look back, I am better because I've been doing it longer. Or maybe it's easier. I'm more comfortable, more at ease constructing a song. But coming up with the ideas is just as difficult. That's why I say I don't know if I've grown.

But you probably have a better understanding of when the structure is right.

Probably, yeah, but that's like saying, "Yes, I've been conditioned."

No, it's just that you're learning the craft.

Yeah, but who's to say what's right? It's all within yourself—and, I guess, within myself I've gotten a better handle on what I feel is right.

When did you first start writing?

I've probably been coming up with riffs ever since I picked up an instrument. It was probably around the time I played high school dances. Just to back up a bit, a main element you're leaving out in my own songwriting is Donn Landee. Donn and I work together at structuring things—I bounce everything off of him before anyone hears it.

So had Donn not been part of the picture from the beginning, Van Halen's sound might have been different?

Definitely. And it would be harder.

Donn understands you pretty well.

You said what I was trying to say. We understand each other well. To the point where the way he makes things sound is basically the way I hear things in my head. This is very unusual.

So what the public hears on the tape is the guitar sound you heard in your head?

Within each given song. I can't say every record was exact. But I'm happy with everything on the last album [1984], and Donn and I worked very much as one on that. We're proud of it because it's something we felt was an accurate representation of what we were capable of. That goes for the band as a whole, too. But it was Donn's and my baby.

You haven't really written lyrics to any extent.

It's not something I'm good at, or something I've spent any time with. A lot of times the way people write lyrics is so personal that nobody knows what the hell the words mean. Dave is that way. I don't even know the lyrics to our own songs, and it's no joke. Because a lot of the stuff is Dave's interpretation of life at that given moment. And even if he experienced it, it doesn't click concerning my life or the state of the nation. [*laughs*]

When you write the music, you must have some idea of what the song should say, lyrically.

I never suggest to Dave what to write the lyrics about. Once he writes lyrics, Ted and Al and I suggest going this way or that way with it. I guess that's why sometimes I don't lean toward his lyrics, because something about them takes away from the mood the music creates, even covers that mood. It might take it to a better place—and sometimes not. Sometimes it takes away from the original feel of what is happening. And I can't exactly say, "Hey, it was sexy before and it isn't now." It's a feeling. Like, how do you explain [*sings opening notes of Beethoven's Fifth Symphony*]? What words would you say to that? When something sounds a certain way, I can't easily picture lyrics with it. Because it's pretty self-explanatory.

Like the opening to "1984"?

Yeah; I couldn't hear any singing over that.

Is a lot of the music you listen to instrumental?

Yeah, but I haven't listened to any of that stuff for at least a year. I don't even have a turntable or a cassette machine in the house.

Do you draw any inspiration from modern music?

Let me put it this way: A lot of contemporary music wouldn't amount to much without lyrics. But I've seen a lot of lyrics and vocals ruin good music, in the same way opera singing over good classical music can do a heavy duty waste number on it. And who in the hell understands what they're saying in opera music? And how does someone in Japan, even though they may learn English in school, know what a person is saying? It's more the feeling. I'm not against vocals or lyrics; it's just a lot of times they rub me wrong.

> I'm happy being who I am—
> I wouldn't want to be
> anybody else.

NEIL ZLOZOWER/ATLASICONS.COM

Do you suggest vocal melodies?
I try and help, yeah. Lines here and there. I never say, "Here's the music. Here's the melody. Fit words to these notes." Because that would be really ridiculous to say. Dave has done some stuff with the music that has been handed to him that has blown me away. Because some of the stuff I come up with is pretty twisted. Seriously. Twisted to the point where if he can squeeze a word or two in there or anywhere, he's got my vote. [*laughs*]

What are your feelings about Dave's solo album?
I think it's something he always wanted to do. I think it's great he's actually doing it. Put it this way—it's something I've always wanted to do, and haven't done. I guess, in a funny way, it explains Dave as a vocalist and lyricist. He did four cover tunes—"California Girls," "Easy Street," "Just a Gigolo" and one other one—yet managed to project his personality through them. I expect it to be accepted by people in the same way everything we've done has been. I've heard it all and it sounds real good. Edgar Winter played a lot of stuff on it, and one of the Beach Boys actually sang on "California Girls." Ted produced it. It's Dave.

Did Dave want any of your input?
No. It's something he wanted to do alone. He actually started doing it when Donn and I were doing the film soundtrack for *The Wild Life*. It's not that he didn't want it, but what's a solo project if you're going to have your band playing on it?

Do you think Dave wanted to have some original songs?
Yeah, I guess. You'd have to ask him that, to tell you the truth. I think these were tunes that Dave feels a part of and always liked and wanted to re-do. I don't think he's out to prove anything. I know it will be good for him personally and his own self-satisfaction when it takes off the way I expect and hope it will. I seriously want the best

Edward at his home studio, 5150, in 1984.

for it, in the same way he'd want the best for me or Al or Mike if we did anything outside the band.

What are your solo plans?
I don't have any plans.

Certainly there must be a record in you that wants to come out.
I'd say there are a few. I haven't thought about it enough or talked to Donn about it enough. I guess in a way I look at it as something Donn and I could do whenever. It's not like something we feel we have to do in order to show anything, or for any other purpose. If the band decided to take a year off, then I could do it. But I don't want the band to take a year off because I'm doing it.

Speaking of vocals, weren't you the band's singer before Dave joined?
Oh, yeah.

Is that when you were known as the Broken Combs?
Broken Combs was the very first. Alex played saxophone and I played piano. This was in fourth or fifth grade. We actually had some original tunes, too. One called "Rumpus" and one called "Boogie Booger."

So you've been playing with Alex since day one?
He's the only one I've ever played with, really.

Was there any competition between the two of you?
No. What I couldn't do he made up for, and what he couldn't do I made up for. That's how he started playing drums. I used to play drums and he'd play 'em better, so I said, "Go ahead, you play 'em if you can do it better." I wasn't going to waste my time proving to my own brother that I could do it better.

Did you play violin?

Yeah, for about three years. Al did, too. That was at the end of elementary school and the beginning of junior high. It was school-based stuff. Al actually made All City Orchestra on violin. I never did.

Did you find it difficult?

I didn't like playing the songs they made me play, so I just started messing around with it and lost interest.

So from the outset, you never followed the rules.

It seems that I didn't. But it wasn't intentional. I remember sitting there, pluckin' on the violin and playing along with the *Peter Gunn* series on TV.

Did your father want you to play violin or piano, as opposed to guitar?

It's hard to say exactly what he wanted us to be; he wanted us just to be successful in life. Deep down he wanted it to be music. He wanted it to be piano, only to the extent that piano is the springboard to ear training—you can orchestrate your fingertips. Each finger is a different instrument. I've learned a lot from piano, and I play it more now than I have because I can play it the way I want to. No one is looking over my shoulder and saying, "No, that's wrong."

You had actual piano training?

Yeah, from age six to 12. I was good. I actually won three first-prize trophies at Long Beach City College for my category in an annual contest. You sit there and practice one tune for the whole year, and they put you in a category and judge you. I think I won first place twice and second place the last time, which kind of showed I was losing interest. [*laughs*]

Did the feeling you had when you won first place mean anything to you?

It didn't motivate me. After I played in the first contest, I sat in the bleachers while they held this beauty pageant countdown; I won and didn't even hear the guy say my name. So I just sat there and they passed by my category because they couldn't find me. And finally, after the recap, they said, "Is Edward Van Halen here?" and I said, "What?" I guess the only thing it really did to me was make me more nervous for the next time. I didn't expect to win or lose. It wasn't like, "Wow, I won. I'm good!" It wasn't a motivation of any kind. I don't see why I won, to tell you the truth.

Did the piano training transfer itself to the guitar?

Oh, definitely, but in a very subliminal way. Because I never learned how to read, really. I used to fool the teacher. I did it all by ear.

It wasn't important to you, to learn how to read?

I guess the reason it didn't get me off in any way was that all it's good for is to learn how to play songs that have been written. And I told you the reason I didn't like violin was that I didn't like the songs we were supposed to play. I guess I was just a snot-nosed kid, and I didn't want to waste the time doing it. I'm sure I could have benefited from it, somehow. I can read, I know what the notes are, but I can't sight-read like Al can. He can open up anything and start playing. I never got close to that. I had to sit there and figure out the left-hand chord and I couldn't handle all those notes.

Was there much music in your house?

Yeah, by my dad. In Holland I went with him when he used to play, but I was so young I don't remember. It wasn't the classical stuff then; he did that before he met my mother.

Your dad supported himself as a musician?

Oh, yeah. As a matter of fact it was the only thing that pulled him through out here when we showed up in this country. We had $25 and a piano.

Did your dad make records?

Yeah. I don't know exactly in what orchestra, but it wasn't "Blah blah blah featuring Jan Van Halen." It was a Philharmonic-type thing, and I have pictures of him standing up and soloing. He's probably on more records than I know.

> I managed to get myself into trouble without having to be rebellious.

NEIL ZLOZOWER/ATLASICONS.COM

Was your mom musical?

Not professionally, but around the holidays my mom and dad jam. My mother has this huge organ with a rhythm box in it, and my dad whips out a sax and they play oldies.

Did your dad push you in that direction?

No, he never discouraged us, but he didn't encourage us, either. I wanted to start playing saxophone, and I kind of felt he didn't want to spend the time. He struck me as being as impatient as I am when it comes to teaching someone something that is very difficult to teach. I don't mean the actual instrument, I mean the feeling behind it. My dad is into that so much that he doesn't even look at sax as an instrument of technical skills—it's secondary to the emotion involved.

How old were you when you got your first guitar?

About 12 or 13. It was a flamenco Spanish guitar, but I didn't really consider it *my* guitar. It was Alex's, and he took classical guitar lessons while I banged away on the drums. I got left with his guitar when he started playing the drums, and decided to get an electric. It was a four-pickup $110 Teisco Del Ray from Sears. I liked it because it had the most pickups. It was fun.

Did you feel anything special when you picked up the electric for the first time?

No, no message from God or anything. I thought it was neat. Some things were easy, some things were hard. I didn't even think about whether it was easy or hard; it was something I wanted to do, to have fun and feel good about doing it. Whether it took me a week to learn half a song or one day to learn five songs, I never thought of it that way.

Did you get an amplifier, too?

I had an amp that was homemade by a friend of my dad's. The plug needed an adapter because it was a phono-plug. I got this weird adapter at Radio Shack and plugged my normal guitar cord into it, and turned the thing all the way up. It made a lot of noise and I started playing it while it was making all that noise. I remember Al walking in and going, "That sounds neat, man, what is that?" It was right around the time of that song, "Blues Theme" [*an instrumental by the Arrows*]. Al said, "Play that," and it sounded identical. It was crappin' out, distorted, nasty, so I guess that was my first exposure to that grungy noise.

When did you become aware of guitarists like Page, Beck and Clapton?

I remember hearing Jimmy Page when a friend brought over the first Led Zeppelin album. And I tripped on it. I might have actually heard that before I heard Cream. My listening history is disjointed to me. I think I might have gotten into Cream, and then dug back to find the Bluesbreakers. I got into blues for a while and then went back to Cream. It wasn't that I was into blues and followed Clapton. I just knew I really dug him and then dug back and really got into a blues kick for six or eight months, or a year. Just jamming with guys, not really playing any songs, but jamming for hours on end, playing the same progression. Falling down the stairs and landing on your feet.

Your technique and style were developing here?

Yeah, but it was just fun to do. I didn't think, If I do this for a year, I'll know this side of it. It was just a very natural thing; I wasn't doing anything for any purpose.

Did you say to yourself at this point, "I want to be a musician"?

I have to think about when that was. I was still in junior high, so I wasn't the rebellious one—yet. Actually, I wasn't that rebellious anyway. I just managed to get myself into trouble without having to be rebellious. I never could get over how

my friends could get away with murder and I was the only one to ever get caught at doing nothing.

What about the story of the time you were caught looking at the exam answers?
Oh, yeah. Actually, I think Al was the one who told me about this, and I tried it and got caught. This English teacher, who was the only teacher I can remember who smoked, would leave the class during a test period and go off to the teacher's lounge and have a cigarette and my friends would go up to her desk and change grades. And I said, "Hell, I might as well do it, too." And right when I'm doing it the teacher walks in. Got nailed.

Did bands like Mammoth come together while you were in high school?
Yeah, ninth, tenth grade. Genesis was another band during that time. Then there was the Trojan Rubber Company. We also used to be called the Space Brothers. When we began playing high school dances and parties we had a hell of a reputation. This is funny because Al, Donn and I were just talking about this the other day—how it seems that only since Dave has been in the band did we get this rowdy and crazy brown cloud hanging over us. But we had it way before Dave was even in the band. Schools wouldn't hire us, nobody wanted anything to do with us, so we had to change the name of the band to the Space Brothers, just so we could play these gigs at a Catholic school.

What kinds of songs did you play?
You name it: Grand Funk, Black Sabbath, Deep Purple, Cream...

Was Gazzarri's [*a local Hollywood club*] your first semi-professional gig?
It was a breakthrough, yes. You know I got kicked out of clubs because I played too psychedelic.

You even had problems getting *into* Gazzarri's.
Oh, yeah! We had to audition there at least three or four times. A guy would come running up in the middle of a song because I was too loud. But I didn't play that loud deliberately; the amp only sounded like an amp if it was all the way up. So I did everything—from keeping the plastic cover on it, to facing it against the walls, to putting Styrofoam padding in front of the speakers.

Were you playing the homemade, one-pickup guitar at this point?
Not right in the beginning. I used to play a Les Paul and a 335, or whatever guitar I had at the time. I also played a Les Paul Junior. That was around the time I got a Strat and the guys didn't like it— "Sounds too thin." I said, "Okay, I'll take care of that." I slapped a humbucker in there and figured out how to wire up the rest of the stuff.

So the idea for putting a humbucker in a Stratocaster body came about as a matter of necessity?
Oh, yeah. I just chiseled a hole in the body. I think I might even have some footage from the Whisky, where I played that original Fender Strat. It isn't the same one that appears on the first album. It's when I realized, Hey, this is neat, and got one from Charvel that was actually a Lynn Ellsworth guitar.

Had you seen or heard anyone reworking guitars like this?
No. I hadn't really seen or heard anyone taking any time to try keeping a vibrato bar in tune either. A friend brought over a bootleg album of Hendrix in concert where he'd grab the bar, and the rest of the night it was out of tune. It was important for me, because for a long time before the Floyd Rose was developed I used a regular Fender vibrato. If you see the guitar on the first

NEIL ZLOZOVER/ATLASICONS.COM

album cover there's no Floyd Rose. I actually did the first world tour with that guitar.

How did you keep it in tune?

That's a tough one to explain. Due to the tension between the nut and the tuning peg, if you bring the angle of the string down it gets stuck in the nut. So I got a brass nut with extra big grooves and no string retainers, and I used to stick the string into the Schallers and wind it upward so the angle would be straight. I'd oil the brass nut, stick the string through the body, wind it a few times and then turn the ball end of the string, because when you tighten a string, you get tension along the string itself. I'd turn the ball so it was straight. That was just another thing in my mind that could cause a rubber band effect—where you loosen a string and it wouldn't come back to where it was. It's hard to say how much any of this had to do with it because certain strings would still go out of tune—they'd go sharp because they'd get caught up somewhere. So you'd have to go and snap it back before you hit the next chord. The thing is, I never hit all six strings when I play a chord; I'm usually doing some take-off on a chord, somehow.

I did this other thing once with a 335. They used to have a real cheap spring metal—bending vibrato on them; SGs had it too. I sawed my 335 in half because I figured I could always land on my feet and make it through a song barre-chording with the low E, A and D strings. So when I hit the vibrato bar it would only be for the high E, B and G strings. It worked great, it was neat. The three high strings would always be out of tune, and the low ones would always be in so I could always chord my way through, somehow. But the guys thought the 335 looked like something Johnny Rivers would play. I actually did that before I got a Strat. I did everything to that 335—belt-sanded it, repainted it, refretted it.

When you changed from the Gibson to the Fender, did your style alter?

I never understood that. What's the difference? One less fret? I can get used to anything. I remember when I got a Strat, everyone was saying, "Oh, going to make it hard on yourself, huh?" Because people like Ritchie Blackmore would say things like, "I play a Fender because it's not the pussy way, it's not easy to play." I made it as easy as a Gibson to play. I never understood why Fenders are harder to play, except possibly that the string length is longer. I never tuned standard anyway, so that relieved a little tension. Try to play to the first record. We tune to A—or somewhere around there. I never tuned; if you can find a strobe-tuner in this studio I'll give you anything you want out of here. I'd just pick up the guitar and, whatever it was tuned to, I'd just tune the instrument to itself and have Mike tune to me, and we'd tune the synthesizer to it. Who made up the rule that an A string had to vibrate at 440, or whatever?

Who made the body of your first guitar?

Boogie. I painted it almost immediately, because it was a wooden body, no finish. It was a junky, piece-of-shit body on the bottom of a stack of other bodies. It was a second. I gave the guy $50 and got a [*Boogie*] neck for $80. I picked up the body and neck and slapped it together; it's not that difficult.

What kind of guitar sound did you hear?

I guess a cross between a Gibson and a Fender—a humbucker sound with a vibrato. Bigsbys were totally childish things. You couldn't really use them to bend pitches; they were a vibrato type of thing.

What I wanted to do was fall off the edge of buildings.

Did you install Gibson frets?

Yeah. I got the fret wire from Lynn Ellsworth and slapped them in. He told me how to do it. A couple popped up here and there so I got out the Krazy Glue.

Do you remember the first time you played the guitar after it was assembled?

Yeah, it was neat. I thought, You can't buy one of these! I felt like I was onto something, and obviously I was.

Why just one pickup?

In a two-humbucker–style Gibson, in order to get a clean, bright front pickup [*neck position*] sound, you'd have to sacrifice the sound of the rear pickup. I couldn't get what I wanted out of the front pickup, and I didn't feel like compromising, so I tended to stick with the rear one. And I tried to make up for a different sound color with playing techniques.

NEIL ZLOZOWER/ATLASICONS.COM

> That was my first experience with **the band not wanting me to play keyboards.**

You used this guitar for the first tour?
Before the first tour—during the Starwood and Whisky days. That was a couple of years before the first album.

Had you always used Marshalls?
I tended to blow them up, so I used an old white Bassman or Bandmaster through a Marshall cabinet. I can't remember.

Were you using pedals?
Same thing as on the first three tours: MXR flanger, MXR phaser and an Echoplex.

What was that hollowed-out bombshell you had onstage?
That's what I used for the tail end of "Eruption." It was a Univox echo chamber. It had a miniature eight-track cassette in it, and the way it would adjust the rate of repeat was by the speed of the motor, and not by tape heads. So if you recorded something on the tape, the faster you played the motor back the faster it would repeat. And vice versa. I liked some of the noises I got out of them, but their motors would always burn out. I don't know how many broken ones I have.

Then they stopped making them.

What were the first tours like?
We went out with Sabbath, Ronnie Montrose, Journey. We did Day on the Green [*in Oakland*] with everyone from AC/DC to Foreigner. It was a hell of an experience.

Were you playing well then, by your own standards?
Yeah, I think so. I wasn't ashamed of my playing. I didn't feel I had a lot to learn. I had a lot to learn about dealing with people, but I felt we held our ground pretty well. If anything, we took a little too much ground. Unintentionally. We didn't think, Hey, we're the best. We just did our gig and whatever happened, happened. Everyone else was a victim of his own bullshit. It didn't come from us.

What was it like, recording the first album?
We didn't have a whole lot to say about much of anything. The songs basically got recorded the way we played 'em. Very few overdubs. I guess it was Ted's [*Templeman, producer*] idea to make it come off as pure and simple and honest as it was live.

Did you agree with that?
I wasn't sure. By the time Donn [*Landee, engineer*] got through with it, I really liked it. I didn't know what making a record was. I guess it was good that we did approach it that way, because when we played live, you were only going to get more.

Did the songs on the first album mirror what you'd been playing live?
Yeah. Things like "Ain't Talkin' 'Bout Love" and "Jamie's Cryin' " weren't on the original demo.

Had you been playing "Eruption" live?
Yeah. Ted heard me practicing it for a Whisky show while I was waiting and he asked, "What's that?" I just didn't think it would be something we'd put on a record. He liked it, Donn liked it, and everyone else agreed that we should throw it on. I played it two or three times for the record, and we kept the one which seemed to flow. I like the way it sounds; I've never heard a guitar sound like it. It's not that my playing was so great, it just sounds like some classical instrument. Donn really made it sound like more than it is, in a way.

Were there any other songs you recorded which didn't make it onto *Van Halen*?
"Loss of Control," which ended up on *Women and Children First*. We wrote "Loss of Control" and "Ain't Talkin' 'Bout Love" at the same time; we were actually making fun of punk rockers. "Ain't Talkin' 'Bout Love" was actually a stupid thing to us, just two chords. It didn't end up sounding punk, but that was the intention.

Had you been in a studio prior to the first album?
We were in the studio once before, with [*Kiss bassist*] Gene Simmons. That was about a year before.

What did you learn from that experience?
I learned that I didn't like overdubbing. Gene naturally assumed I knew that was how it's done. Ordinarily, I would noodle between chord lines, and I had to fill in those rhythm spots on the tape. And I'd say, "Oh, I can't do that, I have to stick to this." So it was rather uncomfortable. When we got in the studio with Ted and Donn, I asked them if it would be okay to play the way I do live. And they said, "Sure, make it easier for all of us."

What was the first song you recorded?
I don't remember. "On Fire," I think. I played the harmonics at the beginning on the A and D strings, one fret down from the E position

NEIL ZLOZOWER/ATLASICONS.COM

[*seventh fret*] on the A string. It's actually not a harmonic; it's just a muffled, dead, weird sound. It sounded kind of machine-like. We wanted a little break between verses, and I said, "This is neat, how about this? It sounds rude."

Did you use a sitar on "Ain't Talkin' 'Bout Love"?

I doubled that one part. It could have been a Coral guitar, but it looked real cheap. It looked like a Danelectro with some kind of stuff muffling the strings back there. I never really knew it was an electric sitar, because it didn't sound like one. It just sounded like a buzzy-fretted guitar. The thing was real bizarre.

How did you get that swishing sound on the intro to "Atomic Punk"?

I used an MXR Phase 90 and rubbed my palm over the pickup. And then during two of the breaks I used a MXR flanger.

You used MXR pedals from the beginning?

Yeah. I don't really use them anymore. I just use an Echoplex.

The guitar shown on the cover of the first album is the one you built?

It's the same guitar I used on all the albums, and all the tours up until the *1984* tour. It was my baby until I started using the Kramers. For a while I was putting Kramer necks on that main guitar [*pictured on the* Van Halen *cover*]. For the second album, I had that black and yellow guitar [*pictured on the back cover*].

Why did you change your guitar?

I don't know why I played that black and yellow one. I liked the way it looked, but I didn't like the way it sounded. Actually, I used an Ibanez Destroyer for a lot of *Van Halen*—the guitar that is on the *Women and Children First* cover. On all the stuff that didn't have any vibrato on it, I used the Ibanez. "You Really Got Me," the rhythm track of "Jamie's Cryin'" and "On Fire," too. It has a PAF on it. It was one of the few guitars made out of Korina wood that you could get, without spending an arm and a leg for an original "V" or something. It was a great-sounding guitar—until I took a chunk out of it to make it look nice, to make it look different. On the cover of *Women and Children First*, it's missing a piece. Boy, did I screw it up.

It changed the sound?

Oh, completely. It ruined it. [*laughs*] It went from sounding like a nice, fat, warm guitar to "What the hell happened?" I couldn't believe it. The sound changed from a fat, Les Paul–type sound to a real weak Strat sound. I thought I'd ruined the pickup when I took the chunk of wood out, so I stuck in another pickup. But it sounded the same—real bad. I think it was because I took the wood out right by the bridge; that's where a lot of resonance and tone come from.

Did the success of "You Really Got Me" lead to your doing another cover for the second album?

I don't know how "You're No Good" came about. I guess it was Ted. He figured, "Hey, it worked the first time, let's try it again." I really don't remember how it ended up being picked. I didn't even remember how the damn song went. We used to play it in the bars, at Gazzarri's, but we didn't play it like that. We played it like the original [*Linda Ronstadt*] record. I know how this version came about, but I don't know how it came about that we used the song. Ted hummed the tune to me, and that's how I came up with the riff; I was just trying to noodle my way through it to figure out the chords. We never listened to the record to learn it. So I don't know if it's right or not.

Was "Spanish Fly" designed to follow-up "Eruption"?

Al and I spent New Year's Eve, 1979, over at Ted Templeman's house. He had an acoustic guitar sitting in a corner, and I picked it up. I was getting drunk—and started playing it. I remember Ted saying, "Wow!" You can play acoustic guitar too?" And I said, "Yeah, I

guess. It has six strings. It's not really any different." And I started doing hammer-ons—whoever came up with that name, hammer-ons?—and I started doing that stuff on the fingerboard and Ted said, "Hey, why don't you do something for the next record on acoustic guitar?" And I said, "Okay, sure." I bought a nylon-string Ovation and used it for that, and I don't know what happened to it. It took two or three takes.

Do you remember when hammer-ons became part of your style?

I think it was around the end of the Gazzarri's days.

Had you heard of anyone playing like that?

Honestly, no. I'm sure people had but I'd never seen anyone.

The sound of the bass on the first two albums seemed to be a little buried.

I guess the sound Mike was getting at the time was either smothering everything if it was too loud or impossible to hear if you put it where it fit.

Did you suggest bass parts?

Some things would just obviously follow the guitar-type of stuff, unless I had a specific bass line. Otherwise, Mike does whatever he feels like doing.

Moving on to *Women and Children First*, did the album mark the first time you used a keyboard in the studio?

Yeah, on "And the Cradle Will Rock..." I had an old Wurlitzer electric piano and I pumped it through my Marshalls. A lot of people don't even know that because it doesn't really sound like a keyboard. That was my first encounter with the band not wanting me to play keyboards—when we did the song live, Mike played it. They didn't want a "guitar hero" playing keyboards, and that kind of ties in with why they didn't want "Jump."

The break in "Romeo Delight" has a real Who-type feel to it. Were you aiming for a *Live at Leeds* quality?

It just kind of happened. I never try to get a certain kind of feeling. I just try to get any type of feeling at all—whatever comes out. [*laughs*] Whatever came out is the feeling I got.

There's also a heartbeat sound on "Romeo Delight."

I think Mike was picking quietly, and I tapped my string against the pickup poles.

NEIL ZLOZOWER/ATLASICONS.COM

NEIL ZLOZOWER/ATLASICONS.COM

No, I've never doubled a rhythm part. I don't know, I just turn it up, I guess. Everything is on 10. We just use cheap Shure 57s.

What is the effect on the guitar on "Tora! Tora!"?
That's backward, and we kicked an Echo Plate [*EMT*] at the end of it. Just for fun.

What kind of acoustic guitar do you play on "Take Your Whisky Home"?
I don't know what that was; just a rented job.

Do you enjoy playing acoustic guitar?
Not really. It's not loud enough.

Isn't there also an acoustic on "Could This Be Magic?"
Yeah, and I played slide on that for the first time in my life. It was kind of funny. Dave and I played together, and I don't know, I guess we had a little difference in rhythm. Like on "Ice Cream Man," Dave played the guitar, that little acoustic part. I just used some glass job for the slide. I had listened to Duane Allman a little bit on *Layla*, but slide is something that has never really interested me. I played in standard tuning.

What is that little piece of music that just fades into nothingness at the very end of side two?
It was something Al and I were working on. I forget what we called it—"Growth," or something like that. We thought that just for the hell of it we'd stick it at the end of the record. And possibly start the next record with it. But it never amounted to anything, so we left it at that.

To my mind, *Fair Warning* took Van Halen to a higher level in terms of record production. There were more guitar parts and more textures. Is that accurate?
I guess. I remember I approached my playing a little differently, where almost every song had an overdub in it, whereas before it was kept way down to a minimum. I wrote rhythm parts that I intended to solo over.

Was that the Stratocaster?
I think that was the Ibanez. I butchered it for the photo session after the record was recorded. [*Sometime after this conversation took place, Edward remembered borrowing an Ibanez Destroyer from Chris Holmes of W.A.S.P. and using it for portions of the* Women and Children First *album.—Ed.*]

At the beginning of "Fools," you play some Eric Clapton–style blues.
Yeah; I don't know where that came from. I think it was Ted's idea to get Dave's voice to sound that way. He wanted people to hear a different side of Dave's voice. That backup kind of blues guitar seemed to fit. That was the Ibanez.

There are all kinds of effects happening in the intro of "Everybody Wants Some!!"
I did kind of a cello thing on the low E string with the palm of my hand. It's the same technique used on "Atomic Punk," but I'm not hitting all the strings.

Did you double the rhythm part to get that fat sound on "Everybody Wants Some!!"?

Are you able to hear in your head what the various parts will sound like when they're finally put together?
Yeah, I usually can tell, but sometimes what I hear in my head doesn't work. But the majority of the time it does.

You did some of the writing for *Fair Warning* on piano?
I did some stuff on piano and some stuff that still hasn't been used—obviously. [*laughs*] The album took a long time to record, because I was getting married and this and that. In the same way *1984* took the longest because the US Festival got in the way. We'd start to record, and then we'd have to make a radio program, etc. Every time we'd start to record it was [*in nasal voice*], "Oh, yeah, we forgot to tell you, you owe us this by tomorrow." The US Festival was actually like a whole tour's worth of work for one hour of playing—everything from the stage setup to rehearsing for it to all the video stuff that we owed them. I know Donn and I were happy to wash our hands clean of that when it was done.

It didn't seem to mar the success of *1984* at all.
No, it didn't. But if we would have had to have the record out at a certain deadline in the middle of that, it would have suffered. But we said, "Screw 'em. We'll put it out when it's damn well ready."

What is the technique you use at the beginning of "Mean Street"?

I tapped on the 12th fret of the low E and the 12th fret of the high E, and muffled both with my left hand down by the nut. I got kind of a funk slap out of the guitar. I applied to guitar what bass players do when they slap. But it's not like I studied it or anything.

The solo on "Mean Street" was very aggressive. Were you an angry young man that day?

[*laughs*] I wasn't trying to be mad, but it just seemed to fit. I think I did do some interesting solos on the *Fair Warning* album.

You decided to try your hand at slide again on "Dirty Movies."

I came up with the melody of it on slide, so I played it on the record on slide. The funny thing was I couldn't get up high enough on the guitar, so I sawed part of it off. I used an old Les Paul Junior that had an SG body style and that one hook...what do you call it?

Horn?

Horn. Yeah, the bottom one was in the way, so I took a hacksaw right there in the studio and said, "Hold this, Ted," and sawed it off.

The bass sound on *Fair Warning* was much better than it was on the previous records.

Yeah. We used different amps, smaller amps—smaller amps usually get a better bass sound.

Didn't you do something interesting with the solo in "So This Is Love?"

Out of six solo tracks, Ted let me mess around a little bit, but I don't think he thought I could get anything. Then Donn showed up and said, "Why don't you try it once?" I thought I was just trying it, but he recorded my composite and that was my first attempt. It's like four solos punched together. That surprised a few people.

Do you go through different feels for a solo before coming up with one that you think will work?

I don't know. It's not an intentional, planned-out thing. Whatever sounds right, I guess.

Do you know if it's right when you hear it back?

Yeah. Obviously, you'd better know if it's right when you hear it back. If not, you're up the creek.

"Sunday Afternoon in the Park" was another song that featured synthesizer.

It was one of those cheap little kid's toys, an Electro Harmonix. It didn't have any notes; you could rub your hand across the whole octave of the board and it would go *rrrrrrrrrrrrr* [*rolls tongue and imitates sequencer line*]. I just blazed it through the Marshalls. It was cheaper than a Casio, and was made of cardboard, plastic and a little sensor keyboard.

Could this have been the seed for "Jump"?

As a matter of fact, I might have had "Jump" by then.

You approached the tracks on *Diver Down* differently than you did those of the first four albums.

Basically, we did more finishing up of individual tracks before moving on to the next.

You did four cover songs on *Diver Down*.

That was too many—four too many. Dave always wanted to redo "Dancing in the Streets," and I remember him giving me a tape of it. I said, "I can't get a handle on anything out of this." I didn't want to do it, I didn't like it. So I suggested "Pretty Woman," because that seemed more a Van Halen song to cover. It was us. I was working on something on the Mini-Moog, and Ted happened to hear the riff and said, "Wow, we can use this for "Dancing in the Streets." So

NEIL ZLOZOWER/ATLASICONS.COM

NEIL ZLOZOWER/ATLASICONS.COM

> **I wasn't trying to be mad with the "Mean Street" solo, but it just seemed to fit.**

picture. We used it on another thing, called "Ripley," that we didn't use on the record. It's a great guitar—a different guitar. You need two amps for it. There's another one that has built-in vibrato, and is actually like a miniature console with send and receive effects, and a patch bay where you can put a different effect on each string. I haven't gotten into that, but I can just imagine having a different effect on each string, panning it wherever you want, and adding vibrato to it. It's basically a guitar for the Eighties—or Nineties.

Weren't you toying around with the idea of building your own amplifier for production?

Jose Arredondo, who works on my amps, and I had some ideas of building our own and selling it as my amp. It'll definitely be an amp that sounds the way I want it to. It will have everything you could possibly want in an amp for good sound.

Your main contribution to the 1984 album was as keyboardist. Any thoughts on that?

No. [*laughs*] It's neat. It's almost like I play more keyboards now than I do guitar. I enjoy playing keyboards. It means you don't have to jump around onstage and have something hanging round your neck. No, I'm joking.

Did the overall success of 1984 give the band more freedom to wander outside the boundaries?

It gave me the freedom to play keyboards comfortably. Now I don't have to worry about what the rest of the guys think other people will think. I never worried about what anyone thinks, except it makes you feel kind of uncertain when the guys worry.

You guys took a chance with "Jump"—a keyboard tune from the guitarist of the Eighties.

"Jump" was not a spontaneous jam. What I was talking about was that live-Cream, spontaneous thing. For one, it would take somebody with a hell of a sense of humor, and they'd have to be a musician to even get anything out of it. I'm talking total darkness concerning format—no form, no song structure, nothing. Maybe someday... At the moment, I'm just writing. We're talking about doing another Van Halen album.

I have a feeling that when we next hear Van Halen they won't be...

The same? Maybe you're right. I guess we'll all have to sit around and wait, and see what that difference will be. I don't really know. It's definitely time to move on. ◼

Ted and Dave were happy—and I wasn't. Because the riff I had for something else got used for a song I didn't even want to do.

Which brings us to the 1984 album. If *Van Halen*, *Van Halen II* and *Women and Children First* represent the first phase of the band's development, and *Fair Warning* and *Diver Down* represent the second level, then 1984 surely must be the third phase?

In a way, it's Phase One of Donn and Ed. Donn and I were very involved in this record. We almost took control, to a point, because it was done here in our studio, and we knew what we wanted. We weren't about to let the album be puked out in any way—especially since it was done here. We wanted it to be an accurate representation of the sound of this studio, and in a way I guess we were proving ourselves—to ourselves, more than anybody. I think everything sounds the best; I like it all.

Did you play any other guitars besides the Stratocaster?

I used a Gibson Flying V on "Hot for Teacher" and "Drop Dead Legs." Actually, I've used a lot of different guitars, recording-wise, but live I usually use just one. I used the V because I needed the pickup switch to do the quiet part in "Hot for Teacher." Live, I used a Roland echo box with a volume knob on it, and I hooked it up to my pedal boards so I could hit the pedal and drop the volume, because I couldn't reach for the knob quick enough on the guitar. That song was beyond any boogie I've ever heard. It was pretty powerful.

1984 was the first album in which you used the Ripley stereo guitar [*an instrument built by Steve Ripley in which each string can be sent to different sides of the speakers through the use of individual string pan pots*].

I used that on "Top Jimmy." It's not really a stereo guitar; it has an individual pan pot for each string, so you can designate where each note you're playing will come out in the stereo spectrum. And I panned each string opposite each other, so the low E string would come out way left and the A string would come out right in the stereo

EBET ROBERTS/REDFERNS/GETTY IMAGES

Reprinted from **Guitar World,** *November 1986*

LES PAUL'S JUNIOR

Twenty-six years ago, *Guitar World* writer Steven Rosen brought together Les Paul and Edward Van Halen for a quick chat. It would be the beginning of a beautiful friendship between the two great guitar innovators.

- - - - -

by Steven Rosen

IN the summer of 1986, Guitar Center opened a mammoth music store on Sunset Boulevard in the center of Hollywood. Edward Van Halen and Les Paul were being honored along with several other musical giants, including Stevie Wonder and amp builder Jim Marshall, as part of the store's general celebration. // It seemed natural to take the opportunity to put Ed and Les together in the same room to talk about what they knew best—playing the guitar. The following is an excerpt from the story that originally appeared in the November 1986 edition of *Guitar World.*

EDWARD VAN HALEN When Leo Fender was doing his thing and you were doing yours, was there ever any competition?
LES PAUL No, not at all.

Did you ever collaborate or talk about your ideas?
Absolutely. Leo Fender would come right over here two blocks away from where we are now on Curson Street, and so would his engineers. They saw the Log and some of the other guitars I had built.

They saw it all happening.
There was never any friction. It was just the opposite. Here's the story of how Leo really helped me: When I developed my first solidbody guitar in 1941, I took it to Gibson and they dismissed it. They called it that "broomstick with the pickups on it." From 1941 to 1951, I couldn't convince Gibson to do a damn thing about putting out a Les Paul guitar. Finally, Leo decided to come out with the Fender solidbody line, and immediately Gibson said, "Find the character with the broomstick with the pickups on it!" And so they asked me to design a guitar. I thank Leo for coming out with his Broadcaster, because it woke Gibson up. Gibson was asleep and Fender was not asleep. That's the way it goes. Fender was the first to market, but I was way, way out front.

It's kind of like the car business—Toyota woke up GM.
Sure. Sometimes you gotta wake somebody up, and sometimes I need some help from my friends. And I consider Leo Fender a very dear friend. To me, I am a Gibson man, but that doesn't make any difference, because I also know exactly what Fender is all about.

With my guitars, I guess I'm trying to bring together what you and Leo have done. There are things I've always liked about Gibsons and things I've always liked about Fenders, but neither one did everything that I wanted, so I've created a combination of the two. My guitar is essentially a Strat body with Gibson humbucking pickups.
I can't always get what I want out of a standard Gibson guitar either. There are so many times that I'll go into Gibson battling to win a point and come out with a compromise. The world is a compromise and so this is what you have to do. It can cost millions of dollars to retool and move something a quarter of an inch. I understand that some of my ideas would cost a fortune.

Another thing that comes into the picture is the preoccupation with how something looks. I've had executives veto an improvement because their wives didn't like the way it looked. They're not thinking about the sound.

I've had that problem with companies I've worked with. I've had difficulty getting something the way I wanted it, because they claimed that other people want it a different way.
Which may be right and may not be right.

Yeah, yeah, but if they want *my* opinion, then I'm giving it to them. I've had to say, "I don't want my name on it if it ain't the way I want it."
I had a case where they put out a guitar without my blessings and I tried to make 'em stop! The funny thing is they didn't stop it, and it turned out to be their number-one seller. [*laughs*] So you can be wrong. Gibson put out an SG, and it wasn't with my blessings at all. They put the pickup in the wrong place, they made the body too thin, and there were a lot of other things I didn't like. So I said, "Clean it up a little bit, will ya, before you put my name on it." So they took my name off of it and continued to make it, and it's their best-selling solidbody guitar to date. Sure, it's a cheap guitar and it doesn't sound as good as the others, but it's a different thing. And it turned out I shouldn't have said what I said.

When you design guitars, do you design them for sound or cosmetics?
Sound. But don't get me wrong, design is important.

It's got to look cool, but it better sound good.
Exactly. It's nice to have both elements. I wanted the Les Paul to look good. That's why we put that finish on it and made it with a [*sculpted*] top, so you could have that clean, violin look to the guitar. It makes it look like a Stradivarius, and you associate it that way, too. ◾

ACE OF BASS

In May 1986, writer Steven Rosen sat with Van Halen bassist Michael Anthony for an extensive interview. In this tell-all, Anthony speaks candidly about his feelings toward David Lee Roth, his role in Van Halen and how the band has changed since Sammy Hagar took on the role of frontman.

by Steven Rosen

There was always this sense of you as being the neutral one in Van Halen.
Well, somebody has to be normal in the band. You got all the extremes. Edward calls me "the Rock" in the band. People take it as you will. It's a compliment. I see a lot going on from one end, which would be Roth's, and Edward's, which would be the other. And I'm just trying to tie it all together and put in my 101 percent and try to make it sound as good as I can.

Would you actually act as a mediator between Edward and Dave?
Yeah, sometimes, but usually it's whoever threw the most punches won.

You talk about having more of an input—how does that translate into your contribution to the songwriting process?
Edward comes up with the riffs and stuff and Sammy is doing 99.9 percent of the lyrics. But what was nice about this album was none of the material was written previous to recording this album. When Edward would come up with a riff, we would all be there and everybody would be working on it. And I think this album is much more of a group album than any of the ones in the past. We actually wrote the album in the studio while we were recording it. That was really neat.

With Edward's bizarre sense of rhythm, is it sometimes difficult to come up with bass parts that groove?
Threes and sixes! That's what Alex says and Alex counts in fours and eights and in the studio, I swear, it's like hell. A lot of the stuff that Edward plays, if I actually think about it in terms of the meter, it's a little hard for me to play. Then on the other hand I just listen to it and Edward will show me what he's trying to do or he'll tap his foot or his hand. I think, Yeah, yeah, yeah. And then I just kind of listen to the riff and some of the stuff when we were recording it, I would listen to the riff different than how he meant to do it. But I'd get my own groove happening with what he was playing and play with it like that.

NEIL ZLOZOWER/ATLASICONS.COM

What is it like playing with Alex?

It's great, actually. Alex and I just clicked when I first joined the band. In the early days when we were playing the clubs, we used to have that kind of Bogert/Appice type of thing. Edward would be soloing and Roth would be singing and Alex and I would be back there. Everyone would look at us and go, "Hey, what you guys doing back there?" It's still the same thing. It's fun. There's a lot of eye contact. Of anybody in the whole band during the live show, I'm like right there with Alex most of the time. I can't stress enough that the rhythm section does play a big part in what we do. We can look at each other and do certain accents without saying anything. He just gives me this shit grin and I know something is coming up.

In the club days before you joined Van Halen you were the bass player and lead singer in your band.

Yeah, before the days of Van Halen. I never really considered myself a lead singer, but when I first started playing, I never knew anybody that was actually like a lead singer to get in the band. And so everyone goes, "Hey, Michael, why don't you try?" Because I was a big radio and record fan and I was always singing to everything that's out. And so I started singing and I've always had a pretty decent range. I've never had any vocal training or anything. So it was mostly for convenience in the early years. It was, "Oh, Mike, he's in the band, he can sing."

Was it hard connecting the playing and the singing?

I've never had any problems playing an instrument and singing at the same time. Coordination-wise, I've always been really good like that. Which was a real load off my mind. Part of the reason I actually joined Van Halen was I didn't want to lead sing anymore; I wanted to play bass. I thought, Ahh, this is great. Here's Edward singing background harmonies and Alex was even doing just a little bit of singing also. Alex used to do a harmony part on "Take Your Whiskey Home." It was the first thing I heard him sing. Alex isn't the singer of life but I thought it was great.

Somehow they asked me to sing this one part that Ed couldn't sing on one of our songs that we were doing back then called "She's the Woman." And Edward was having problems with it and I guess they had written that song right before I entered the scene. They said, "Mike, why don't you try that?" and I sang it and it was, "Oh, Mike's got all the background parts."

Not that I wouldn't sometime down the line like to do some lead singing. I guess if I put all the time and effort into trying to make it really good that would be different. Sammy does that; he's always on top of his voice and drinks the right kind of things. You can't guzzle Jack Daniel's all night and then expect to sing lead. Those kinds of singers don't last long at all.

The high school band you were in before Van Halen was called Snake, right?

Yeah. I was the lead singer and bassist, Steve Hapner was the drummer and Tony Codgen was lead guitarist. It was your basic three-man power trio type thing. I knew of Ed and Alex from school because I was taking some music classes at Pasadena College and Ed and Al were taking basically a lot of the same classes but we were taking them at different times. Plus you got the little ring of bands in a certain area and everybody kind of knows each other and goes, "Oh, yeah, I know the guys in that band." I always liked their band; I

When we're onstage whether we're opening up or headlining, to us, we're headlining.

always liked the way Edward and Alex played. I didn't care much for Roth, to tell you the truth.

And one night we opened up for them at Pasadena High School and I got to talking with them. I guess they blew their P.A. up or something, so I let them use ours. I was watching them on the side of the stage thinking, Yeah, these guys are great. Roth strolls over to the side of the stage and he's wearing some little vest type affair and his hair was frosted some weird color. He goes, "Hey, well, how do you like my boys?" And I go, "Get the hell away from me you homo."

You had never met Dave before?

No, that was my first encounter with Roth. It was after that show I played with them that I was talking with Edward and I was saying, "Yeah, it might be kind of cool to jam some time." As fate would have it, I heard they were getting rid of their bass guy and through a mutual friend that Edward and I had in school, he recommended me to Edward. His name was Mike Francis Chini. He was like a real good school chum of ours. Through him he suggested me to Edward and gave him my number and I can't remember if it was him or Alex that called me and asked if I wanted to jam with them.

You went to their house and played with them?

I came down and it was a little garage they were rehearsing in and Roth never even showed up; it was just Edward and Alex and we played all night and it was really neat because it was the same type of magic for me anyway as when Sammy first played with us. You get together and you jam with people and you can play blues in all 12 keys and it's like, "Yeah, nice." Or else you start playing one thing and we'd just go off and keep playing and playing. Al had a case of Schlitz Malt there and we had a few beers and kept playing and playing and it was like, "Hey, you want to join the band?"

That must have felt pretty amazing.

I brought one of my brothers with me because I was nervous. I was playing backyard parties and these guys were playing Gazzarri's in Hollywood. So I brought my brother along with me for kind of moral support. And Ed asked me, "Hey, would you like to join the band?" I looked at my brother and he was really blown away and I'm just going, "Well, yeah!" So that's how that happened.

What high school did you go to?

Arcadia High School and Edward and Al went to Pasadena High School, I think. So I knew them. In fact before they even got Roth in the band, I remember going to a carnival that our school had and I heard this band playing Grand Funk Railroad's "Inside Looking Out" off the second album and there was this guitarist [*mimics guitar playing the riff from the song*] and I'm all, "Wow, this guy sounds exactly like [*Grand Funk vocalist*] Mark Farner." So I go to check out the band and it's Edward and Alex.

That was the first time you ever saw Edward and Alex play?

That was the first time I ever saw them. And they had their bass player, Mark Stone, and they were out there playing. Edward had this headband and this long hair in his face and the same thing with

Alex. Everything that they played, Edward sounded exactly like the guitarist he was copying. It was like, "Wow, this band is heavy competition here in the area." I also heard them a couple of other places, a couple other high schools. I was always amazed that Edward, even back then, played like that and sounded like that. That band was like, "Wow, these guys are really happening."

That was just the trio?

Yeah, and Edward was lead singing.

But they weren't called Van Halen when you saw them?

No, I believe at the time they were called Mammoth. It was right after Dave joined that they changed to Van Halen. And I think it was about a year later when I joined the band.

Mark Stone was the bass player until you joined?

Until I chimed in.

Dave also had his own band before joining Van Halen. Did you ever see them?

No, I never saw his band. I heard of them but I never saw them. I guess his band was a little more outside. Roth was always into the haircuts and the dressing and the show and stuff like that.

That was Red Ball Jets?

Yeah, Red Ball Jets. I know [*guitarist*] Terry Kilgore was in that band—I became good friends with him later on through Edward and Alex. But I basically didn't know anybody in that band then. Oh yeah, he had a drummer and I think his name was Dan Hernandez, who I know now.

What are your early memories of the first rehearsals with the band?

The first big impression that really stayed with me was when I went to the first rehearsal. I go to tune up and Edward says, "No, we tune down." A lot of the riffs that Ed was coming up with was a lot of suspended A chord type riffs. And to enable Roth to sing to that, he had to tune his guitar down. I looked at my bass, I tuned down and looked at the string. I went, "Oh man, I can see major problems developing here." I had to raise my action and get heavier strings and actually after a while look for basses so I could tune down that low. It was a pain in the ass.

So you were actually tuning down to accommodate Dave's range.

I went, "Wow, can't this guy sing a little bit higher?" I never really considered him a good singer by singing standards. Great showman, great actor, great comedian, that was his forte. Live I sang more than he did; I sang a lot of his parts that he didn't want to sing. Sure you've got to give up a little of the musicianship to put on a good show live. There are a few things that I could do but I don't do. Sometimes I make mistakes; I'm only human when I'm jumping around.

It was like Dave sacrificed so much. Besides him singing the verses, which he never sang live anyway, all the choruses and the other lit-

NEIL ZLOZOWER/ATLASICONS.COM

tle parts that he would sing I had to sing because he's gotta make this jump. So I was very unimpressed with the fact that he sang as little as he actually did. Or a lot less than the public was led to believe.

Edward always said Dave had to be on everybody. Why do you think that was?

I think partly because of his lack of being an actual singer/musician. Plus he came from a broken family and I guess the way he is he's always had to buy his friends and stuff. A lot of people that were close to him who worked on our crew and stuff, yeah, because he paid them well. But as soon as something would happen, he'd turn around and kick them right in the ass. He always had to be, "Yeah, they love me don't they? Don't they? Yeah, yeah."

Shit, whereas the rest of us were just trying to be ourselves and we consider ourselves musicians. I didn't really care about dressing up that much; I'd still get out there in jeans and a T-shirt and I could kick their ass the same way. Same thing with Edward and Alex.

Dave did bring a certain focus to Van Halen.

Yeah, there was a certain flair that the normal Joe in the crowd, that wasn't the guitar hero or whatever, and wanted to actually see something, would go, "Yeah, check this band." Besides the fact in our earlier years we partied a little bit harder than we do now. He had a certain flash and people would be curious as to, "Gee, who is this?" That did bring a lot of the Van Halen crowd to become our fans. Now we're finding out it's not the opposite but not as much as we thought it was in the past. Everybody would be worried, "Well, Roth's gone, there goes at least half our fans."

Were you concerned when Dave did leave?

I knew there were a hell of a lot more fans that liked the band part of this band. Not just because all the guys would be flipping Roth off live and shit.

By the time you joined the band, they were already playing Gazzarri's?

They had just started there recently. In fact one of their last shows they knew they were playing, Edward had me come out there and I listened to them and I watched their show to see what they were doing. It was really challenging for the first few months because they had a real big repertoire of songs. They weren't into rehearsing for a few months and not playing anywhere before getting back onto it. Almost every rehearsal, I was learning at least three or four songs every day.

What kinds of covers did they do in those early days?

Whatever was out at the time; a little bit of ZZ Top, a little bit of Grand Funk. Basically what you'd hear on the radio. They'd do a few Top 40 things I can't really recall.

They already had some original songs written?

I heard a demo that Edward gave me of four songs that they were doing originally. One was called "Take Your Whiskey Home" and another one was "She's the Woman." The solo part in that ended up as the solo in "Mean Street." "Simple Rhyme" they were doing. They were also doing "Out of Love" but I don't know what it was called back then. And a lot of other bits and pieces that ended up on the earlier albums.

NEIL ZLOZOWER/ATLASICONS.COM

There were a lot of nights that I can truthfully say I didn't enjoy going out and playing.

Were they already doing "You Really Got Me"?
We weren't doing that until a while after I was in the band. We also did the Kinks' "All Day and All of the Night."

The band started playing other clubs besides Gazzarri's?
We were playing every single bar joint. We had Top 40 stuff that you played and we even started doing some Ohio Players stuff. We were doing "Fop" and K.C. and the Sunshine Band, like "That's the Way I Like It." We were singing the horn parts. That's the kind of stuff to get into the club then after that you start edging in your own original stuff. Around the third set and once we knew the people were in there and they're becoming big fans of the band, then we start poppin' off some of our own stuff. But we played just about every club around the area.

So you were slowly moving toward doing all originals?
After a while we thought, Hey, we could do this the rest of our lives or we could start playing more of the original stuff. I remember we finally decided, "Let's make that cut, let's do it, let's go for it." No one was making money; the old musician's soup thing: ketchup and boiled water. Edward and Alex bought a couple of pairs of overalls and they were painting street house numbers on the curbs. They go up to houses and people would think they were working with the city and they'd charge five dollars. They'd do that during the day and my father was playing like their father. My father was playing in a polka-type band.

What did your dad play?
He plays trumpet. He played professionally a long time ago with Kay Kyser in Chicago and stuff like that. It made it a little harder for me to get into the business because he knew about all the problems and stuff. He never made it as a famous musician but he played with a lot of famous people.

He was reluctant to have you go into the music business?
Oh, yeah. When I joined Van Halen I quit school finally because it was just too much to play every night. I quit college. I majored two years in psychology because he didn't want me to do music. Then he said, "Okay" and I started to major two more years in music and right before my A.A., Van Halen was starting to really take off. At this point, Edward and Alex weren't really going to school; maybe a music class here and there. Roth was out and so I quit and my old man kicked me out of the house. I was living with my sister for a couple of weeks. Of course after our first tour I bought him a car and he's my biggest fan now. I played polka stuff with my old man's band on weekends. I played some trumpet or else I'd play bass with him to earn a few extra bucks that way.

Was there one specific show you played with Van Halen where you could really feel the momentum was turning?

We did a show at the Golden West Ballroom in Norwalk, California, with UFO and I remember Rodney Bingenheimer was the big emcee. It was the first all-original set we ever did as a band. And this place was like 1,500 to 2,000 people and we came off great. We did a great show and the people loved it and Rodney Bingenheimer really liked us and kind of helped us get our foot into the Starwood. We were still playing Gazzarri's every now and then but at that point [*Bill*] Gazzarri said, "Hey, if you're gonna be playing down here, you're not gonna be playing at my club." So we said, "Well, there's the break, no more Gazzarri's."

The Starwood became a huge steppingstone for the band.
We played there and that eventually led to the Whisky. There were these little concert impresario-type guys around town who would throw little shows and they decided to throw a show at the Pasadena Civic.

That must have been a huge step up from the club gigs.
I remember the first show we did there we did an all-original show. We had an opening act and then we did three hours because we thought it was like the Led Zeppelin type of thing. "We're gonna go out there and give them a full night of Van Halen." And we took a little break in the middle for a costume change. We were still playing some clubs every now and then between these other shows. And we were doing backyard party-type things when parties were real big, like 2,000 to 3,000 people at a backyard party. It was amazing back then.

The band was really growing.
We felt the more that we got out there and played, the more people are gonna watch, a bigger following, and we can't help but be noticed by somebody sooner or later.

Was Dave a team player at this early stage?
Everybody had the same feelings in the band. I didn't know Dave as well; I didn't know if it was because I didn't want to. With him and me it was always more like a business thing. Sure we'd get drunk and have a beer and talk but I never actually went out and partied with Roth. I did a lot more with Edward and Alex back then. But everybody wanted the same thing back then. We were just real hungry for it. Roth would find the gigs and be the charmer and take our picture around or our tape. Alex would be the guy like, "We want $125 a night or we're not gonna do it." Alex and Dave were more the business, getting the gigs and stuff.

Rodney Bingenheimer was sort of a trendsetter in Hollywood and you said that he took Van Halen under his wing. Did he have anything to do with Warner Bros. coming down to see you at the Starwood?
He didn't really have anything to do with Warner Bros. coming

to see the band really directly. But they knew through him that we were playing there. How it came to Mo Ostin actually coming out there, I don't know myself.

Do you remember that night at the Starwood?
Oh yeah. We were playing and just being our regular selves. They weren't paying at the Starwood anymore really; they were going to have to cut paying any local acts and just pay name bands. It was like one less place that we could play now because we couldn't afford to drive out to Hollywood every night with gas and road crew and stuff. It was kind of rainy that night and we thought, Nobody's coming, and after we finished we were upstairs and it was like, "How do you do? I'm Mo Ostin and this is Ted Templeman." Our mouths dropped to the floor and I remember Mo saying he really loved the way we played "You Really Got Me." And Ted said, "I'd like to do a demo with you sometime; get together in the studio and do a few songs and see what develops." Next thing I know it was contract time.

Then what did you do?
We scrambled out and got ourselves a lawyer that Roth's old man got us. And it just progressed from there. Marshall Berle was thrown into it because of his connections he'd had in the business. All of a sudden we're signing management contracts [*with Berle*], record contracts and actually when we signed we didn't go into the studio for a long time because Ted was doing a Doobie Brothers project.

What year is this?
We were doing all of this in '77 and there were some months before we got into the studio. So we played a couple more Pasadena Civic shows and a couple of people from the company came and saw us play, including Carl Scott [*Senior VP Artist Relations*]. He saw us and actually saw how we went off live with 5,000 people watching us and we got them all jacked up more, too.

Edward has said that Warner Bros. never thought Van Halen would be a huge band for the label. Do you have any feelings about that?
In a day and age where there were a lot of gimmicks, a lot of flash and stuff like that, they saw the flash in Roth and this band. Templeman believed in the band because he saw the potential for a real good band and I guess it was at that early point where they were possibly going to try to match Sammy with us back then. It was never brought to our attention. I guess contractually and stuff like that it never came to be. We did have to really work hard for what we attained.

It was a sort of gradual process for the band?
It grew steadily. When the first album came out, every single day was record stores, handshaking and radio stations. It wasn't like they had thought that we were going to be really big, like Boston or Foreigner. Instantly those bands were there. Our album grew steadily and so did our popularity, but it wasn't an instant jump to the top. We went out for a six-week tour that turned out to be a 10-month tour in '78—we looked ragged after we got home. I've got pictures just coming through the airport in the middle of the tour on our way to Japan. We stopped at LAX, said hi to the girlfriends and the family for an hour, and whoosh, back on the plane to continue the tour. We had the road tan happening, white as a ghost.

What was it like making the *Van Halen* album?
It was weird in the fact that, for me personally, I hated the sound that I got on the first record. With the exception of a couple songs like "Jamie's Cryin' " that I used a pick on. When I was playing with my fingers back then, I was all over the place. I was slapping the bass because that was my style. When I was in the studio, I didn't know to play a certain way to get a good sound. And Templeman was infatuated with Edward's guitar playing and really made that known on the first album. I acquired this nickname called "Cannonmouth." A

NEIL ZLOZOWER/ATLASICONS.COM

We were blowing Sabbath off the stage every night.

lot of our harmonies we sang live out of one mic; Edward and Dave would be right on the mic. And here I'd be all the way in the back of the room against the wall.

You really didn't have any idea of how to get a good bass sound?
It was so totally different than anything I'd ever done. Because I was sitting there slamming my bass. Not to really slam Ted but I wish he would have worked more with me too on that first album because if you can hear a lot of clicking and slapping on the bass. Which was after a lot of compressing and limiting and stuff like that after it was done. I had a lot to learn playing in the studio.

Did Edward seem like a natural in the studio?
He's one of the few people that I've played with that is always real natural. Whenever he picked his guitar up, the nervousness was gone; he just played. He was Edward Van Halen. Whereas I've played with other guitarists and they'd either try to be real show and flash or gritting their teeth real hard because it's supposed to look

like total pain playing. And Edward picked up the guitar and he was himself.

Because Edward's guitar was a main focus on the first album, did you ever feel intimidated by playing with someone with that kind of talent?
Hey, when I first picked up a bass guitar and started playing, my old man was the first person to tell me this: "Bass guitar, you're in the background. That's it. You stand next to the drummer and keep your lines going and that's it. That's all you'll ever be." When I first started playing bass, I loved it so much that I didn't care. Sure, you want to be known no matter how much somebody will try to say that that's not the reason. Everybody wants to be seen and sure, I felt that way a bit, too.

There was something just playing with this band. I had played in bands with two guitars but I always went back to the three-man band because to me there was a lot more spontaneity, a lot more eye contact, and you could actually play more than bands with keyboards and stuff.

NEIL ZLOZOWER/ATLASICONS.COM

Then everything has to be planned out and I hated to think back then about "Ten bars of this and then we make the change to that."

But playing with Edward and Alex was just so natural. Of course, I had to simplify a lot of things so Edward could go off and do his thing. There was never any jealousy or anything like that. I was having a great time.

What did you think of *Van Halen II*?
The second record could have been produced better, I think. There was a lot of good material on it. Boogie stuff, but I think it came off too soft. It didn't have the edge of the first one. We were going through weird things with Templeman because he was trying different things. "Well, let's try to get some sweet harmonies happening" and stuff like that and, to me, the album just came out sounding a little too sweet. It could have been a little harder.

Ted Templeman did have a good rapport with Dave.
Oh, yeah, he was Roth's mentor when it came to lyrics and melodies for the vocals. For the most part Roth had his few licks down that he did and he did them over and over again all the time. So Templeman was in there saying, "Well, let's try and sing this line." And of course if I was there anything they sang, I'd eventually work a harmony to it.

Do you work that way with Sammy?
I still do that. Like on *5150*, everything we were working up, I'd do a third harmony to everything he sings. I'd do the easiest thing and then other harmonies come out of that.

The harmonies were always a big part of the Van Halen sound.
That's a big part of what sets us apart from a lot of other heavy metal so-to-speak bands. Because you've got one singer screaming away all the time. It makes it more than just a hard rock band with a lead singer screaming his head off.

Did you identify at all with bands like Mötley Crüe or Ratt?
I never did; I don't feel any kind of identity with bands like that.

Were Quiet Riot around when you were playing clubs?
Yeah, in fact they opened up a show with us at Pasadena College once. That's the only time that they ever played with us. That's when Randy Rhoads was in the band. I don't know if [*singer*] Kevin Dubrow was in the band back then. I don't remember too much; I remember this band was going to open up for us and the guitarist was good. Of course he was good; he listened to everything Edward played. He played everything Edward played. [*laughs*] I just remember that they all looked pretty boyish. They had all the real nice styled haircuts. I don't know if they had any makeup back then. No matter what the competition was back then, we never really took it that much to heart. When we're onstage whether we're opening up or headlining, to us, we're headlining.

By the end of the first tour, you were already headliners.
Yeah, we headlined some shows in England and in Japan. We did a big European thing and played some small places in Belgium. I can't even remember; we played so many small little shitty halls. Then we came back and we opened up for Black Sabbath for a little bit and ended the tour like that. It was after their *Never Say Die!* album. At that point we knew that we'd be headlining after that because we were blowing Sabbath off the stage every night. But a bunch of nice guys to work with. Everybody in the world has opened up for those guys that have become popular too. Everyone from Nugent to you name it.

You're obviously as close to Edward as anybody, but when he

brought in some new wrinkle like a keyboard or something, were you excited by that? Was it like, "I wonder what he'll do next?"
Edward was always coming up with new things. If it wasn't that, it was a new effect he was using onstage. When I first started playing with him, he was using a wah-wah on some stuff. That was right after the big Jeff Beck craze and all the guitarists were using wah-wahs. But even like what he was doing with that was so much different than anything else I heard people do with a wah-wah pedal. It just blew me away. Not that he was really all that much into effects. He always had his Echoplex set for just his right amount of slap but he was always coming up with different things. Whether it be throwing a wrench into a piano and trying to play it with a wrench laying across the strings or stuff like that. That's Edward Van Halen. He's just so outside when it came to his instrument and the way you approach music.

Is it really true that Dave didn't want to do "Jump" when Edward first showed him the song?
No, when he first heard it he was like, "Keyboards in our band? No way." In fact, in the early years of the band, I had sideburns that went down lower than the bottom of my ear and he used to get on my case about that. "Rock stars are clean shaven," he would say. I proved

NEIL ZLOZOWER/ATLASICONS.COM

NEIL ZLOZOWER/ATLASICONS.COM

the middle of the stage and Roth you stay there and I'll stay here and sing my harmony parts here.

What were those last rehearsals like?

It got to the point where we were at rehearsal and he was onstage and you could tell. It was, "Hey, these are your buds, this is the rest of your band. You don't have to pull that shit on us; you don't have to act that way toward us." Sure, it's fine to get out onstage and act that way and let everybody else think you're like that. But we know what you're like. He'd come doing the strut into rehearsal.

What did you think when Dave recorded the *Crazy from the Heat* EP?

I remember we were going to Europe and we were sitting the airport and he played us the tape, the EP of the songs that were going to be on the album. I thought it was pretty shitty that he'd always get on Edward's case because he was being approached to do different things like "Beat It" and all kinds of different things. And Roth was, "If this affects me, I want to know." And then all of a sudden, one day he goes, "Hey, I got these four songs that Ted Templeman and I are going off and doing." It was, "Wow, what is this guy's trip?" Was he testing the waters to see what he could do on his own? Now that he's finally got an inkling of what's going on within the band.

He plays us this tape and it's like, "Mmm, yeah, good." I wasn't going to tell him to his face that I thought it stunk. I wouldn't buy anything like that myself. I'm like, "Well, this is really gonna give Van Halen fans a good shot in the arm as to what this band is now?" He's doing four loony cover tunes that have nothing to do with any kind of music that we're doing. And personally everybody I know who bought or listened to the EP was saying, "Hey, is this just some kind of joke thing that he wanted to put out?" And he's, like, serious.

What happened after the European tour?

I think it was two days after we got back from the 1984 tour and did the "Hot for Teacher" video. That was the first video where we actually used a lot of production, a lot of people; kids and stuff like that. We used a high school in the Hollywood area—I think it was Franklin—and after that everybody just basically shook hands and said, "Let's take a vacation now until the end of the year." Which was like two or three months. Then the shit hit the fan.

them all to be wrong. Actually with him out of the band, it gave the rest of us more input. It transcends into the live show too because it's like more of four people playing in the band now rather than the Dave Roth comedy hour with his backup band.

Roth was pulling his big trip. Ed, Al and I would be warming up, we'd be playing, and all of a sudden Roth comes in. "Session may begin now." Edward wanted to leave the band in 1980 and it was basically Alex and I who said, "Hey, there's this big thing that's growing now and let's see what we can do with it." Alex was a big influence on Edward to help him stay in the band.

Did you have a sense that everything was coming to a boil?

We knew things were happening, that things were gonna happen pretty soon. We went out and had a great tour, a lot of fighting on the road that year. It was kind of like business time; that tour really started to seem like it was a business. There were a lot of nights that I can truthfully say I didn't enjoy going out and playing. Only because I did not want to go out there and have to deal with Roth. He'd come up to me during a show while I was singing and throw his arm around me and go, "Yeahhhhh!" And I'm looking at him going, What the hell is this guy doing? He's putting a show on for me too? What? You want to show the audience how we really feel about each other? Okay, we draw a big line right here in

Looking back at life with Dave, how do you see it now?

I swear to God, when it comes to thinking back about it I'm just numb. At this point I can't ever even imagine him being in the band live anyway because it's so much more enjoyable playing now. This whole thing brought Ed, Al and I closer too. I think we're better friends now than we've ever been.

You're happy again.

I'm the happiest I've ever been. I've got a daughter now, the band is happening, and I've got three great friends in the band. Touring this year and just looking at Edward, there's no pressure. Like the *1984* tour, he'd always be in the tune-up room and not the hospitality room because Roth would be there. Now he hardly goes into the tuning room to play. He warms up and stuff like that but I can sense that he doesn't feel like he has to go in there to be away from anybody.

Do you think Dave is happy?

I don't know. He's got enough money, but he'll never be happy.

PAGE 089

Reprinted from Guitar World, *September 1986*

ON THE ROAD

David Lee Roth was out, Sammy Hagar was in, and *Guitar World* was there to get the inside scoop from Eddie Van Halen.

- - - - -

by Steven Rosen

You seem so happy with the new band, Ed.
Dave always said I'm not happy unless I'm unhappy, so to speak. And that's a crock—I'm happy as hell and I'm coming up with some great stuff.

Will you ever look back at those years with Dave and regret that it all fell apart?
Hell no. It was a blessing in disguise. When we get nominated for a Grammy and win, I'm going to thank him. [*laughs*] I'm serious.

Have you heard any of the music Dave's been working on?
I hear it's good. [*Bassist*] Billy Sheehan is a bad mother—one of the best around.

They may have songwriting problems—Dave doesn't write and [*guitarist*] Steve Vai doesn't write those types of songs.
And Billy writes heavy metal riffs.

So he'll have to find outside writers.
He already bought some tunes from Steve Lukather. Steve is such a nice guy, he actually asked me, "Hey, do you mind?" I said, "Hell no, I don't mind." Billy Sheehan kind of asked me the same thing. And I said, "What do you think? Dave just left the band and he wants the

hottest guns in town to replace us." And he asked, "Well, hey, we're still friends, right?" And I said, "Sure, I don't care. I got no beef with you." Actually, I've got no beef with Dave either—it's just that he really hurt me. You know? That's what it boils down to, and that's why I was so pissed off in the very beginning. At the height of our career—you work at something for so long, and all of a sudden someone just pulls the plug on you. That's kind of cruel.

Did Dave really pull the plug?
Yeah, he quit! We weren't getting along, but we never did, basically.

Didn't you want to leave the band several years ago?
Yeah, four years ago. During *Fair Warning*. I wanted to quit, but I stuck with it, and that's what burns my ass even more. If I would have quit then I wouldn't have spent an extra four years putting up with his attitude. I mean, hey, the guy's creative, okay? But he's a lousy human. Trying to live with the guy on tour...you ask anybody that's gone on tour with us, and they'll tell you he'd yell and scream for his apple in the morning. Or ransack people's rooms for the *Playboy* somebody borrowed the night before.

Power trips?
Oh yeah. And Noel Monk [*the band's manager at the time*] was his

> ## Sammy bought a house two doors away from me and we get along great. It's like we've known each other all our lives, really. Very close.

goddamn puppet—did everything he wanted. And that's partly why Al and I wanted to change; we wanted a manager who managed the band—not someone who did only what one person said.

Had you left during *Fair Warning*, it would have been...
...different, sure. Well, let's put it this way: The end result is, I'm very happy now. Whatever it took to get where I am now, I'm very happy.

Was "Dreams," from the new album, played on the MIDIed piano?
Yeah, I think so. We never even got to work with Dave on that; we rehearsed maybe for a total of a week within a month's time.

So he had heard some of the new material?
Oh yeah, I had "Good Enough" and "Summer Nights," and we'd begun work on "Dreams."

It appears from *5150* that your writing has moved in new directions.
It's constantly changing, I guess. I don't really know where inspiration comes from—or where anything comes from.

Was there any worry about the ideas not being there?
Oh, not at all. The way I feel about it is, Sammy and I are in tune with each other. I have to say that, often, opposites will attract. Dave and I were completely opposite in our backgrounds and music, our musical styles and what we enjoyed listening to. And sometimes that works. The friction creates something.

Like with the Who?
Yeah, but there Pete Townshend writes everything. With Sammy, we're the same—and it seems to work better. So the theory that opposites attract is not valid in this case.

Did you listen to many singers before finding Sammy? I know you listened to [*Australian vocalist*] Jimmy Barnes.
And he's doing well. I got a tape from him, and it's the same record he has out now. I don't know; he's a great singer, but I didn't think he was right for the type of music that I write.

Did you think that having Hagar in the band would make it sound like Sammy Hagar's band? As opposed to some unknown vocalist?
I think Sammy Hagar's work on this record is like nothing he's ever done. No, I never thought we would sound like Sammy Hagar, because I'd be writing the music, and my music doesn't sound like

Sammy Hagar music. I pulled some vocals out of him where even Sammy kind of flipped and said, "Whoa, I didn't know I could do that." I guess we pushed each other.

Was Mick Jones important in that area?
I produced all the vocals with Sammy except for "Dreams," because Mick was on tour. Mick helped out a great deal in organizing things. You know how I am—"Hey, let's work on this today. Nah, let's work on that." Or whatever. He really helped pull it all together and polish it up, so to speak. Mick [*Jones, producer*] changed a few things and he offered a few ideas. He and I wrote "Dreams" with Sammy. The song was completely different than it is now. Originally, what is now the verse part was actually a part of the solo section. The same parts were still there but they were juggled around. And he tore a hell of a vocal out of Sammy on that one. Mick is great to work with, a nice guy. We call him "The Duke." A proper English guy.

How did you meet him?
I met him through Sammy at the MTV Awards. Now, it's in our contract that Warner Bros. has the right to refuse producers. I wanted the band to do it by ourselves with Donn, and they said, "No." So what we did was, we went ahead and did the whole record anyway, and then brought Mick in and had him kind of oversee it. But I think Warner knows now that I'm not the flake that I've been reputed to be.

Billy Gibbons had a similar experience—no one was sure about the idea of bringing synthesizers into ZZ Top, and he just asked for a chance to be heard. I think they believe him now.
Yeah. [*Warner Bros. production executive*] Lenny Waronker was a great help. He came down and heard stuff that we were doing, and he was flattened—floored. He said, "Whoa, I didn't think you guys could pull it off." After he heard a couple of cuts he said, "Go for it," even before Mick showed up. Then he began to trust us.

How come you're not working with Ted Templeman anymore?
Actually, he came to one rehearsal. We showed him about four or five tunes. He made notes and everything, but he had a commitment to Dave. He didn't know when he was going to be working with Dave, and it just so happened that we wanted to start—we wanted to get rolling. I got sick of sitting on my ass. It's funny that Dave says we wanted to sit on our butts and stay at home and not tour and not work. I sat on my thumbs waiting for him for eight months, and I didn't want to wait another month to start recording. And Ted said, "I have a previous commitment," and we said, "Okay, fine, see ya later." It wasn't like we split. I'm not saying we'll never work with

Sammy Hagar (left) and Eddie Van Halen in 1986.

ROSS MARINO / RETNA LTD. (PREVIOUS SREAD AND THIS PAGE)

him again; it wasn't that type of thing. Ted is great, but he took Dave's side. But it was obviously because he committed himself to Dave after his *Crazy from the Heat* thing.

Perhaps Ted has more control over Dave than he does over you.
Oh, sure, yeah. With us he'd have to put up with me. [*laughs*] Which I don't know if he's into too much.

Logistically, then, if Ted could have produced both the Roth and Van Halen albums, you would have agreed to that?
[*pauses*] Probably, yeah...I don't know, it's hard to say. Put it this way, he was our number one choice because, obviously, he knows me and Alex and Mike and Sammy very well [*Templeman produced Hagar's* VOA *album and the Montrose records*]. And he and Donn have worked together for years. So it just seemed like a logical thing. Whatever differences there may have been, it could have worked. At least from my end.

I get the impression that you wanted to be more involved in *5150*.
Oh, sure. The way we did this record is basically how I would like to have done all the previous ones. And I think that's another thing that maybe drove Dave away. For *1984*, I built the studio, and began wanting to do things a little more my way. I guess I turned some people off; I created a little friction, though unintentionally. I built the studio for the benefit of all of us, for the family, for the band. But I guess certain people didn't look at it that way, because Ted sure didn't dig working up there. Even though he loves the sound of the place, he just kind of looked at it like if I got pissed at him, I'd kick him out of my studio. [*laughs*] Though I'd never do that. If anything, Dave is the one who did that.

Do you wish you could've worked with Dave the same way you do with Sammy?

I don't know. I don't know if I could have gotten out of Dave what I can get out of Sammy. I don't know if this is slandering Dave, but Sammy is just a better singer; he can do anything I ask him to do. Whereas Ted has a much better handle on what to get out of Dave, because Dave is kind of limited, vocally—range-wise and stuff. I don't know if that's a bad thing to say. I don't know how that is going to look in print. But I mean, hey, Dave has a unique voice and a unique style and also has a very strong idea of what he wants. So does Sammy, but I just pushed him a little further. Gave him a little confidence and said, "Hey, hit this note." And he'd go even higher than the note I asked him to hit. He'd be blown away and it would be great.

Did the fact that Sammy had greater facility than Dave lead to a change in your approach to writing songs?
Sure. Like in "Why Can't This Be Love?" there is this part [*sings the middle part where the voice doubles the keyboard*]. I would never have attempted to ask Dave to do that.

The *5150* sessions felt good with Sammy?
More than anything. He's changed my life. Seriously. He bought a house two doors away from me and we get along great. It's like we've known each other all our lives, really. Very close.

Why wouldn't Dave allow himself to be a friend?
I don't know. Well, in the beginning I guess we were, kind of. But he was always too much into being a star. And that is what he is. I'm a musician, he's a star. A musician doesn't want to go and star, direct and write his own movie. We were really just different people. Sammy and I are a little more the same. A little more human, so to speak. [*laughs*]

Is the feeling in the band now similar to what you experienced during the very early days of Van Halen?

EBET ROBERTS/REDFERNS/GETTY IMAGES

TIME & LIFE PICTURES/GETTY IMAGES

Dave pretty much always had that edge to him—that attitude. I don't know where it came from—insecurity, or having to prove something to his peers. But he always had that uncomfortable kind of attitude of never letting his guard down and opening up and actually letting you inside him. Sometimes I wouldn't know what kind of mood he was in. He's so moody sometimes that you only converse when he wants to. Whatever. Not much more about him, okay?

Okay. Getting back to the music, did you really meet Sammy through Claudio [*Edward's and Sammy's mechanic, who is pictured at the outset of Hagar's "I Can't Drive 55" video*]?
Yes. Claudio gave me his phone number. He's a friend; I hang out at his shop sometimes to talk about cars. And I told him, "Hey, man, our singer left, he quit." And he said, "Hey, well, I just talked to Sammy today and he's coming to town." So he gave me Sammy's number and I called him up.

What was Sammy's reaction to the call?
He said, "Wow, this could be something!" He wanted to come down to meet us first and see what kind of condition we were in. Because he'd heard some horror stories about my being...way out there, a space case. And he came down and said everything he heard through—well, I won't name any names—but he said, "Man, what's with those people? Why are they talking dirt about ya?"

He came down with Ed Leffler, his manager. We said, "Hey, we want a band, we don't just want to do a project with you. We want you as a permanent member of the band." First we had a little business meeting, just because he wanted to know what we wanted—to see whether it was like the album he did with Neal Schon, or what. We told him we wanted a permanent member. He came down the next Monday and we jammed, and that was it. The first tune we did was "Summer Nights." And from then on it was just straight up. In 20 minutes we had a complete song.

Was the energy similar to the feeling on *Van Halen*?
I can't compare two totally different worlds, totally different atmospheres. Better. In the very beginning, the first album, I was very intimidated by never having been in a studio—it was all new to me. I learned over the years what I want and how to get what I want.

***5150* sounds more crafted than I thought it would be; I expected it to be...**
Rawer?

But if you examine it, it is the next logical step up from *1984*.
I wouldn't say more "crafted"; crafted, to me, sounds like put-together. I'd say it's a little more polished, a little shinier. But not for the purpose of being more mainstream; that just happened to be the music I wrote. And that's the way it transferred to tape. I'm not about to deliberately screw something up to give it an edge. Everything has that garage-band energy, but it's polished—we haven't lost that rock and roll soul.

Was it an easy album to make, in terms of putting the songs together and knowing when they were right?
A breeze. Beautiful. We never put anything down and then decided to change it. We'd write a tune, put it down, and say, "Yeah, that's it." We might've edited a few spots if a part was too long, but the elements were there.

Some time ago, you said you knew that whatever you did would be judged by what you had done. Did this make you nervous when you were recording *5150*?
Oh, sure, it gave us all a little more *ooomph*. Made us try a little harder.

With regard to the session, were the keyboard parts recorded before the guitars?
Yes, I did all the keyboards first, alone, and then Al put down drums

and Mike overdubbed bass. And then I overdubbed guitar. On "Love Walks In," I played by myself without a beat at all. Seriously. Ask Donn. It was tough for Al but I wasn't that far off. I wanted the chorus part to retard a little bit, and you can't do that with a click track—it would've sounded too robot-like. So Donn and I said, "Forget it, we'll just wing it," and Al managed to play it. "Dreams" was done with a click track. I used an old 1912 Steinway seven-foot B Grand MIDIed to an Oberheim OB-8.

Is that an acoustic guitar at the beginning of "Dreams"?

Yeah. It's a new Kramer Ferrington acoustic guitar with a thin body and an electric guitar neck on it. They sent me the first one. It sounded great, so I had to use it on something.

Did you use the Steinberger guitar on the album?

Yeah, with the Trans-Trem. I used that on "Summer Nights" and "Get Up." It's an amazing guitar. You can hit a whole chord with a whammy bar and it will go up or down in tune with itself. So "Get Up" sounds like I'm playing slide, but I'm actually using the wiggle stick.

You were initially wary of the guitar, I understand.

Well, that was because I'm used to a piece of wood, and this thing is like plastic. It was kind of alien to me. I had to change a few things to make it sound right. For instance, I had to use my amp differently—I had to use a bassier input. But I talked to Ned [*Steinberger*], and he made some different pickups. They're still EMGs, but they're a little warmer-sounding than the ones he sent to me.

I noticed that the solos on the record sound kind of angry.

Angry? Maybe subconsciously, I don't know. But I think they're just sleazy. Kind of slimy-sounding—you never know where they're going to go. They just slip and slide. It's like the old "fall down the stairs and hope you land on your feet" thing. Whatever fits.

Yet the solo on "Love Walks In" is so lyrical.

Yeah, I planned that out. I had a melody in my head and it happened to fit. So I said, "What the hell? I might as well use it."

Does Sammy play any guitar on *5150*?

No, I played all the guitars. Live, though, he does the solos on the keyboard tunes.

Years ago, didn't Ted Templeman want Sammy Hagar to be Van Halen's singer?

I remember hearing something like that. The thing is, Dave has always hated Sammy. I never understood why. We did some shows together—the Oklahoma Jam, and Anaheim Stadium with Black Sabbath and Sammy Hagar—and I always went over and said hi to Sammy because I dug him from his Montrose days. And Dave would always talk shit about him: "Ahhh, that little mother, he ain't got nothin' on me." And I'd wonder, Where's that even coming from? Why the animosity? And what Dave says is true—they never even met. Sammy never said a bad word about Dave until Dave started saying shit about him in the English press. I never knew where he was coming from; probably a slight case of jealousy.

I wonder what Van Halen would have been like with Hagar as the original singer?

Ummmm, I can't speculate. Maybe Sammy would be doing a movie right now, and Dave would be in the band. [*laughs*] You never know. Seeing how Sammy is blonde, too, we—Alex [*Van Halen, drums*], Mike [*Anthony, bass*] and I—figured our purpose was to make lead singers into actors, movie stars. It's just a joke.

5150 is your first Number One album—how does it feel?

It shows me that music overpowers bullshit. Dave and I wrote a lot of good stuff and made a lot of good music together, but I guess the clowning and the show biz part of it only works and helps so much. What's on that tape is what counts. Bottom line. And our going Number One proves that.

Then you think that coming off a huge album like *1984* would not have ensured success had you made a poor album?

It would have bombed. But I think we made a good record—a solid record. There's not a song on there I don't like. On previous records there were tunes like "Dancing in the Streets." Come on! That's not me. A funny thing, though: We've played it live—on guitar. Just for fun. We did that in South America when we toured. Maybe if I'd played it on guitar on the record it would have been better. The riff on the record actually was taken from a song of my own, that I was in the midst of writing. Ted heard it and said, "Hey, let's use it for that."

Looking back, what moments stand out for you? Was *1984* one of the high points?

It was both a very high and a very low point, emotionally, for me. Since it was recorded at my house, I got a lot of flak from producers and from Dave. In a way, that made me work harder and, in a way, it turned me off to working with those people. So what I did was work at night after everyone split, and then the next day play stuff for them. They're the type of people who, I guess, like to work from noon to 6 P.M., break for dinner, go to sleep at 11, and wake up at noon again. You know what I mean? I'm not that type of person. And they knew that all along. So I guess it scared the crap out of 'em when I built the studio. Because, hey, I'd wake up at five A.M. and want to play. If an idea pops in my head, I want to put it down. You don't put off an idea until tomorrow. I basically wanted to work when I wanted to work, or when I *could* work. I can't just flick a switch on like Dave obviously can. I can't do it that way—at least not creatively.

But after *1984* came out and they saw what you were capable of, wouldn't they allow you more control?

I don't know. I think it scared them more. I don't think they were ready to work with me under those conditions again. I think it was that, along with getting rid of our manager, that made Dave just say, "Well, screw you guys, I'm taking off, too." But we didn't do anything wrong. Alex and Mike and I were just sitting there saying, "Whoa! I thought we were doing great. What the hell is going on?" Here was Noel, our manager, suing us. What happened was, he wanted to renegotiate. He sent us a letter saying, "I want more money." We said, "Let's negotiate," but he wouldn't accept our offer. So we didn't fire him, he quit. And since Dave and he were so tight, so to speak, when Noel split he must have really felt he had no more control over me, Alex and Mike. Particularly since Al and I started opening our mouths for a change and were sticking up for what we thought was right. *1984* proved we were right, and so did this new one—not that we were even out to prove anything.

5150 has more keyboards than any album you've ever done, and it's been the most successful.

And what's funny is that Dave was basically against keyboards. Like Billy Gibbons and his, "Hey, you're a guitar hero, nobody wants to see you play keyboards." They had a mental block.

We never even got together long enough to see what he would have come up with for the stuff I was writing. He was too busy doing interviews for his solo career when we had a record to make. He'd call up and say in a gravelly voice, "Ah, I can't make it today, man," and I'd call the office and he'd be doing interviews.

What did you think of *Crazy from the Heat*?

I think it was a novelty item. He didn't write any of it—it's full of songs written by other people. In my mind that's an easy way out, because the songs he did have been hits already. Ted has always said, "Hey, when you redo a hit you're halfway there, because the song's

EBET ROBERTS/REDFERNS/GETTY IMAGES

I never thought Dave would quit— I thought he'd wake up.

been proven." But that's not my way of thinking; I like to do my stuff. That isn't to say I like my own stuff better. But if you have ideas, why be a bar band—why not take a shot at your own stuff? I had enough of playing other people's music in clubs for seven years. Now that I have the chance, I want to do my own now.

You made a Number One album with no videos.
Yeah, that's true. The reason was that we didn't have time to do even one. And on top of that, my main reason was that since Van Halen used to do such extravagant, loony videos, I didn't want people judging the new face in the band and the new unit by what they saw on some script. I wanted people to see us as we are onstage first. After it was known what we were about, then we could goof off and do whatever we wanted in videos.

Warner Bros. and everyone else wants a video out of us. Our next single is going to be "Dreams." We won't have the time to do a video for that unless we do a live one, so that's probably what we'll have to do. Live is actually the best way to go—it presents us the way we are, not engaged in doing some goofy stuff. The goofy stuff is fun to do, but we didn't want people to get their first impression of us that way.

Do you see yourself doing some outside producing?
Sammy asked me to produce his next solo album. And it's going to be fun. I dig working with Sammy, it's great. We come up with stuff so quickly, it's incredible. And he can step out a little and do all kinds of stuff—like writing folk tunes on acoustic guitar. Show a side of himself other than the Red Rocker.

Will the next album show that side?
Yeah. One thing Sammy's record won't be is anything like Van Halen. I'm not going to write or play on it; I'll just produce. Because if I write and play, it would sort of sound like Van Halen. And it's not a Van Halen record. I don't want anyone to have the impression that it is—or that he left the band and we're looking for another singer.

Speaking of outside projects, did anything ever come of your desire to work with Pete Townshend?
I feel really bad about that. I think Pete Townshend is really pissed off at me. We talked—actually he never called—but he sent telegrams. I tried calling him back, and he telegrammed to say he doesn't like to work in the States, that he wanted to work in England. That kind of threw me a curve, because I was kind of planning to do it in the studio at home. But that wasn't the main reason. He wouldn't have been able to start until November of last year because he was doing his book and his solo album [White City]. I was tired of waiting to do something. Also, here are Alex and Mike, who I love, and who are my friends, and who I've been with for years—I couldn't exactly just leave them out. Pete and I never really discussed how to approach the thing, whether it would be Alex and Mike and me or what. I just hope he's not mad at me because I never got hold of him to tell him, "Sorry, I can't do it." I lost his number. I tried to call Phil Chen, who originally got the number for me, and I lost his number, too. You know what a slob I am. I write something down on a matchbook and I light a cigarette and throw the pack away. So Pete, if you read this: I apologize.

Weren't you also trying to work with Patty Smythe?
I actually hit her up to possibly join the band and be our lead singer. I just bounced the idea off her. She wasn't sure she could deal with three guys, or something along those lines. And she has a happening solo trip.

Another thing that was bounced around was doing a record with me writing all the music and getting different singers—Joe Cocker, Phil Collins, Mike Rutherford—a different vocalist on each track. But Alex talked me out of it. He said that would be just a one-shot project, and it made me realize, Yeah, I want a family, I want a solid thing.

The thing is, I never thought Dave would quit—I thought he'd wake up. The things that he said were so weird. He asked how long the album was going to take, his attitude was [*mimics sarcastic tones*], "Hey, man, I've got better things to do, how long is it going to take?" I told him to count on about a year from starting point to album release—writing for a couple of months, recording for three months, and then all the red tape crap of mastering, album covers, T-shirts and all that. And he put it in the press like I just wanted to rot in the studio for a year. We recorded this album in three and a half months—we started in November and by March were on tour for nine months. And he told the press that these so-called "married men" with their Lamborghinis didn't want to tour, but only wanted to do some summer shows. He was the one who suggested not doing a record and just cashing in on the summer circuit. And I said, "What? I don't want to go on tour without any record." He said, "Hey, man, it don't matter." I said we had to do a new record.

The thing is, he's more into money than I am. I'm into making music; I'm a musician. And I love people liking what I'm doing. He's the businessman, not me.

How has Donn responded to the new face?
Actually, it was Donn who said, "This is it." Seriously, that one Monday night we jammed, we played for 20 minutes and Donn flicked the talk-back button and said, "I never heard you guys sound that good."

Even Michael and Alex's sound has improved.
Oh, yeah, it's a new fire. I'm not saying we couldn't have done a good record with Dave, but I think he started believing the attitude he started copping, the "Hey, I'm God" syndrome. To the point where his hat wouldn't fit his head anymore. I was still willing to put up with it.

I'm curious: how did Valerie respond to all this?
She was pissed off, too, because she knew I wanted to quit years ago when we were doing *Fair Warning*. He used to pull shit on her, telling me, "Tell your old lady not to say this and that in the press about you." Bullshit stuff. I said, "Hey, I'm normal, and whatever you are, you are. Don't tell my wife not to say the way I am." I could write a book about the stuff that went down, and none of it had anything to do with music. The guy just did not treat anybody like a human. He was like Idi Amin or Muammar Qaddafi. ▪

EBET ROBERTS/REDFERNS/GETTY IMAGES

Reprinted from Guitar World, *February 1990*

THE MONSTER OF ROCK

He sparked an Eruption—and an aftershock of monumental proportions: Edward Van Halen, *Guitar World*'s player of the decade.

- - - - -

by Joe Bosso

"LOOK AT THIS MESS!" Eddie Van Halen takes in the barren and dusty confines of the apparent wreck and ruin of 5150, his beloved recording studio/clubhouse. Where most men find rest and rumination in neighborhood bars, Eddie has for years sought refuge in this, his hangout-joint to end all hangout-joints. Here he stays up late, pours back some Buds with his buds, and plays his videos. Here, too, he cranks it to hell and back, capturing bits of genius on two-inch tape.

But at this moment he couldn't nail a solo banjo track in here, let alone the monstrous sonic booms for which Van Halen is universally celebrated. 5150 is being remodeled, so everything's been stripped away, sawed-off, gutted. Amps, effects racks, consoles—all gone. Construction will take at least a few months to complete, at which time the dream-like studio will sport a new look and house, and, for the first time, a drum room. But on this picture-perfect Hollywood day, poor Eddie Van Halen looks like a man without a country.

"What are you gonna do?" he shrugs, accompanying *Guitar World* Associate Publisher Greg Di Benedetto and I out onto the driveway. "That's where we're building the new house." He motions across the small valley that lies between the Van Halens' modest (by rock star and TV actress standards) one-bedroom digs and their soon-to-be constructed palatial estate. Half-a-dozen workmen are engaged in various digging, pouring and pounding activities. The house glistens in the L.A. sun and, while unfinished, looks like an architect's dream. Eddie grins a grin as only he can, lights a cigarette and assesses the situation with characteristic amusement. "The thing's taking twice as long as it was supposed to, and it's costing six times as much!"

MARTY TEMME/WIREIMAGE/GETTY IMAGES

If I wanna play keyboards or if I wanna play tuba, I'll play it.

EVH looks good: California-tanned, thinner than he's been in recent years and sturdy. He pads about the room, casually comfortable in beyond-baggy jeans, T-shirt and well-worn sneakers, with the cool, somewhat oblivious air peculiar to the mega-rich. For all that, it almost seems as if Eddie Van Halen is really just another guy, a bud—a dude. Perhaps that's how he likes it—as if the Porsches, Mercedes and Lamborghinis cluttering the driveway and parking lot could disappear tomorrow and it really wouldn't be that big a deal. Most successful rockers would take a journalist down to the wine cellar, but Eddie's idea of fun is showing off his motorized skateboard ("You can really clock yourself on the head when you fall off that thing at 35!"), or visiting his guitar room for a little stroll down memory lane.

"This place is a bit of a mess, too," he explains, running his hands along the bodies of guitar after guitar, as if to reacquaint himself with his collection of lovelies. "I don't usually keep 'em in cases because guitars are meant to be functional, you know?" [Later in the day, as we prepared to drive into downtown L.A. for a photo shoot, Eddie took his famous Frankenstein striped Strat and his 5150 guitars, among others, and tossed the whole bunch in the back of his pickup truck like they were two-by-fours. As each guitar landed with a loud thud, I gave Eddie a somewhat astonished, quizzical look. He simply grinned. "I don't use cases for these either!"]

"There's the Electro-Harmonix over there," he points to the keyboard just near the stairs. "I used that on 'Sunday Afternoon in the Park.' And there's the Destroyer I used to use," he says, pointing to one of the guitars hanging on the wall. "That was the one on *Women and Children First*. Oh, and here's what a Variac looks like!" Eddie's enthusiasm waxes as he holds up a harmless-looking electrical device that is most commonly used to dim wall lights. Eddie, of course, has for years routinely slapped them in his amps to better modify the voltage.

He ambles back outside where, plopped on a picnic table near the swimming pool, he reflects on a career that has not only brought him worldwide acclaim, fame and untold wealth, but, more importantly, has forever changed the way people play and listen to the electric guitar.

Although it is difficult today to imagine modern rock guitar without Eddie's influence, surprisingly, when the group that bears his surname released their debut album in early 1978, they were perceived as something of a throwback. While most popsters were caught up in the minimalism of post-punk, with its arty blend of end-of-the-world nihilism and Euro-style detachment, along came this louder-than-loud Southern California band of party-crazed Gypsies, blowing up amps and pillaging any u nsuspecting town in their path. Their equipment was crude and their songs were empty-headed supplications to the pleasures of limitless wine, women and song. At a time when Gary Numan and Kraftwerk were setting the trends and the electric guitar was taking a backseat to the synthesizer, it appeared that this band didn't stand a chance.

Enter the round-cheeked Eddie Van Halen. As fast as he could unleash a flurry of dizzying harmonics, he tapped his way into our hearts, the first to infuse the electric guitar with genuinely new blood since Jimi Hendrix. For even if the young Van Halen's recording career had ended the moment he unplugged after tracking the seminal solo *tour de force* "Eruption," his place in the history of the electric guitar would have been assured. With this much-imitated instrumental, Van Halen single-handedly introduced the hammer-on to a generation of guitarists. Not only did "Eruption" serve to usher in an important, unconventional artist, it signaled the rise of something greater than that—it launched a movement. Overnight, the stakes were forever altered—and guitarists worldwide knew it seconds after their needles hit Van Halen vinyl.

In 1982 Eddie, by then an established rock star (a term he despises), received a call from producer Quincy Jones, who was working on a red-hot rock and roll track for a Michael Jackson album. Would Eddie come to the studio and lay down a solo? Sure, thought Eddie, why not? Might be fun. David Lee Roth had always frowned upon the idea of Eddie playing on other people's records, but hey, this was a Michael Jackson record, so Van Halen fans certainly wouldn't be interested—probably wouldn't even hear it. Eddie grabbed his guitar and split for the studio. Once there, he found that he liked what he heard, the driving song called "Beat It." The track was pretty much all there; Steve Lukather had recorded most of the guitars, and all that was needed was a solo—a hot one, to really make the tune cook.

After making the crucial suggestion that he solo over the verse section rather than the breakdown, as was originally planned, Eddie winged it. The solo would turn out to be Eddie's most popular and most analyzed work of the Eighties. All fired up, whooping and swirling, growling and shrieking, it is the product of a heart meeting a mind and connecting with the unknown.

It's a head-turner, all right, and for more than the obvious reasons. Eddie Van Halen was the perfect choice to play the solo, and his cameo spot on a Michael Jackson song carried repercussions that went far beyond guitar heroics. Until then MTV, still in its infancy, had maintained an unwritten rule against the airing of "black"-oriented videos. Although the network somewhat reluctantly agreed to air Jackson's "Billie Jean," it was a hollow victory, a response borne more out of record company pressure than popular opinion. But Eddie's star-turn on "Beat It" demolished the color barrier with stunning, decisive force. MTV had to respond. And it didn't end there. Suddenly, FM hard rock stations, which primarily catered to white suburbanites, were deluged with calls for "Beat It." Across the country, white males, who ordinarily would never dream of buying a Michael Jackson album, were doing so in record numbers. At the same time, black stations—the last places one would expect to hear searing, burning, heavy metal guitar—were wearing out their copies of "Beat It."

It seemed appropriate that Van Halen's brilliant and influential solo was the product of a whim. For this artist is—musically and personally—the personification of explosive spontaneity.

Eddie sits back in his chair, lights another cigarette, and grins

KEVIN ESTRADA / RETNA LTD.

Eddie Van Halen in the dressing room of the Whisky A Go-Go in West Hollywood, CA, on May 29, 1977.

that grin. The greatest guitarist in the world is ready to talk about 10 incredible years gone by.

What is the single thing you're most proud of having accomplished in the last decade?
I guess it's that I introduced and came out with a slightly different style, and that a lot of people have picked up on it.

The song "Eruption" changed everything practically overnight.
Well, that's kind of what I'm saying, that I changed the way people played the guitar, you know? I mean, you see everybody doing it, and they weren't until I did it. So it's kind of obvious. It's not like I'm on an ego trip or anything.

What's your take on the L.A. band scene nowadays? How has it changed since you played the clubs?
I think, in a funny way, that Van Halen kind of paved the way for that, too. When we were playing the clubs, there was no room for a bunch of long-haired, platformed, goofy-lookin' fools! [*laughs*] It was real hard for us to get into the clubs. It was always [*in gruff voice*], "You're too loud, your guitar's too psychedelic, etc." We used to get fired because you'd have to play five sets of Top 40 stuff, and we'd only have one set—which we'd play for the audition. We'd get the gig, play our one set of Top 40 songs, and then start playing our own stuff. Halfway through the second set the club owner would be screaming, "Hey! Get the hell outta here!" So we'd have to start playing our own gigs.

A lot of bands do that nowadays—the self-promotion thing.
I'm not really too familiar with the club scene today. I don't even know where to go if I want to go to a club. I don't get out much.

There's the pay-for-play thing happening.
Like at [*Los Angeles club*] Gazzarri's? I heard about that. You have to pay to play?

Bands have to pay something like $1500 to play.
I'll tell you, making 75 bucks a night isn't much better! [*laughs*] It sure isn't enough to buy equipment. I mean, Alex and I used to go around and paint house numbers on curbs to make extra money.

Who are some of the players that have impressed you during the past decade?
Well, there's Satriani and Vai. They're excellent players. [*pauses*] I don't really listen to anything! I'm always wrapped up doing my own stuff, always writing.

Any lesser-known players?
Well, there's this band I'm producing called Private Life. And Danny Johnson, I love the way he plays. He's got that Louisiana blues sound, but he can also have the fire of Allan Holdsworth. He's got the vibe I really like.

One of the things you pioneered was two-handed tapping.
I don't know if I was the first one to do it. I mean, I'm sure that somebody else thought of it, too! [*laughs*]

Nevertheless, people equate Van Halen with pyrotechnics. You brought it to the masses.
Right. Funny thing is, I think I've mellowed out in my old age. I see a lot of people using it as a trick, but to me, it's just the way I play. It's not like, "Oh, oh, I'm gonna do a trick now!" I mean, you see these other guys playing and it's, "Watch this!" A trick. Like a vibrato bar—I don't use it as a trick, but as a way to play. I think I've gotten a little tastier through the years. I don't play as recklessly; I'm a little more melodic. I guess I'm much more into songs and songwriting.

Does it bother you that people have focused so much on the two-handed tapping technique? That maybe some other aspects of your playing have been overlooked?
Yeah. I mean, whether I tap or not, I'm still a good player. If that's all I'm known for, then goddamn...

There are so many technicians around now, people who can really wail. But there are very few sonic innovators—people whose sound is instantly recognizable.
I think that comes with time. When I first started playing, I was like—"brrrrrrrrr!"—as fast as I could go, too. It was fun. But as you mature a little bit, you see there's no point to it, and you start using your technique to bring out your style.

NEIL ZLOZOWER/ATLASICONS.COM

When did you notice that you were progressing on the guitar a little faster than your peers? When did the term "guitar hero" begin to be tossed in your direction?
Probably when our first album came out.

But before then, there must have been people who said you were a pretty hot player.
Well, yeah, when other people tell you, sure. Okay!

You've always acknowledged the mistakes on Van Halen albums. What are some of the most amusing examples?
All kinds of stuff! I don't think there's any one song of ours that's done right all the way through. [*laughs*] Sometimes I'm out of tune

a little bit. I heard "Where Have All the Good Times Gone?" on the radio the other day, and I'm doing these harmonics...missed 'em. I kinda chuckled.

But most people would've removed their mistakes.
Especially nowadays. Everything's so technically advanced. I'm not really a perfectionist, in that sense. I'm more for a vibe.

There was a pretty good goof in your cover of "Oh, Pretty Woman." You forgot part of the bridge.
Yeah. I screwed up! [*laughs*] I never bought the record, I didn't know how the song went, so it was, "I think this is how it goes," you know? And so we did it, and realized later that it was wrong. I met Roy Orbi-

son at Farm Aid. I don't even know if he knew we did it. You know, everybody was pushing for cover tunes on *Diver Down*, so I said, "Well, let's at least do 'Pretty Woman'—it's got a riff, unlike some of the other stuff we were doing.

Did you intend to go right from "Intruder" into "Oh, Pretty Woman"?

Oh, that was an afterthought. We'd done the video for "Pretty Woman" and needed something else for it, so we went in the studio and just tagged that on. I was drinking a beer—that's me sliding the can on the strings—"A-rooo! A-rooo!"

Van Halen's sound on your first couple of records was very much that of a raw, live band. But this has changed somewhat. Now it's a fuller, more produced sound.

Yeah, well, the main thing in the beginning was that I had never

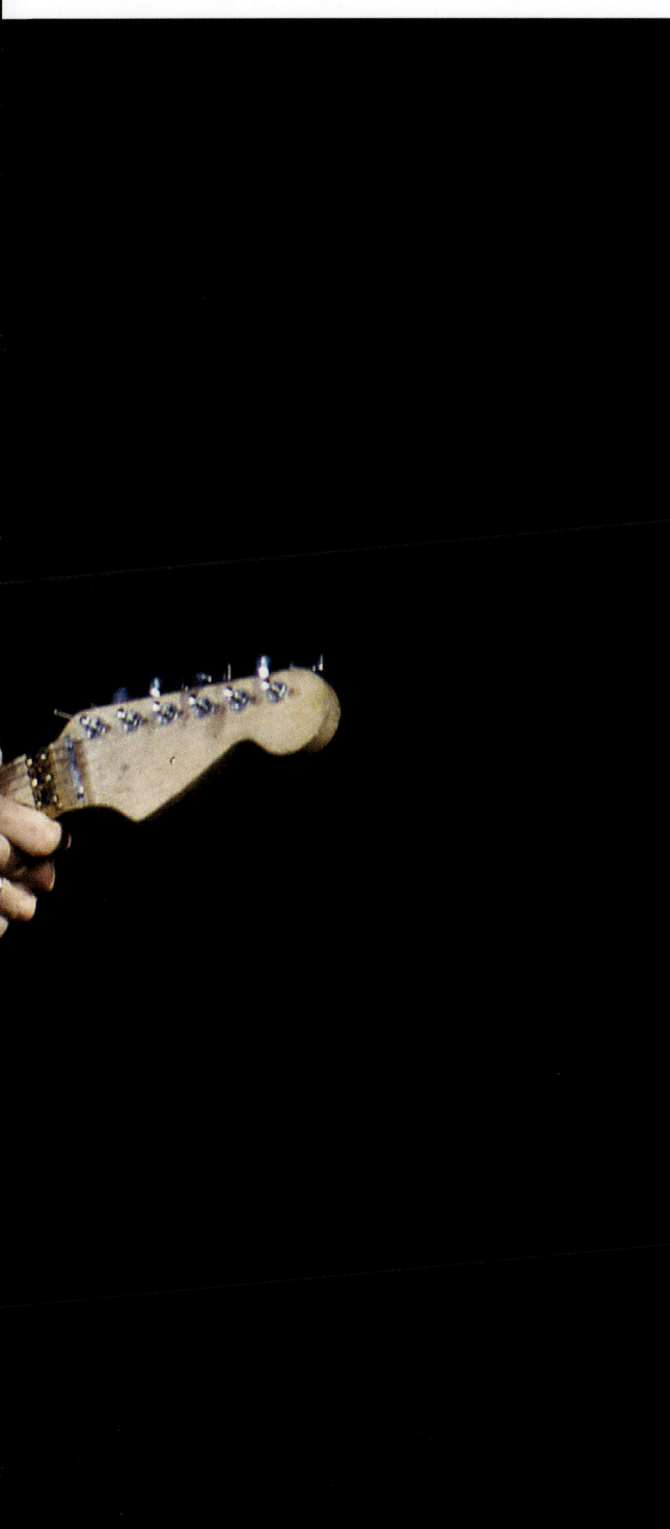

FRANK WHITE

rhythm part underneath. I guess we're just getting better at recording. The technology has advanced so much since '77!

Do you think your guitar sound has changed any?
Believe it or not, I'm using the exact same stuff I always have. I have an old baby Marshall. And Kramers, which I started playing around five or six years ago. I don't know, I just turn everything all the way up! I used to use those old MXR Phase 90s on all the solos—it's kind of a cool sound. I don't use that much now, though. I have a rack that looks like computer shit, but I don't even know what's on it. [*pauses*] The only thing I use is a little bit of delay and a couple of Harmonizers. It's not a real tight echo.

You've been successful for some years now. How do you fend off complacency, the whole "rock star" trip?
See, all I do is make music. I don't go out. I just sit up here on the hill, in my studio. I've always been that way, so nothing's different. A lot of people want to be successful so they can go out and party and have fun. But to me, making music is the fun part. I'm a weirdo! [*laughs*] I mean, that's what you saw out there [*points in the direction of the studio*].

"Beat It" created such a buzz. How did your involvement with that song come about?
Quincy Jones called me up to ask if I wanted to play on Michael Jackson's record.

Of course, at the time, Michael Jackson wasn't the pop icon that he is today.
I didn't think he was. But when that record came out, it sure was a big one! It was really funny. I was out back, and something was wrong with the phone. And you know, there's always people calling me. So I said, "Hello?" And there was this guy answering, "Hello?" We couldn't hear each other, so I hung up. And then the call came again: "Is this Eddie? It's Quincy, man!" And I'm like, "Who the hell? What do you want, you asshole?" [*laughs*] So finally he says, "It's Quincy Jones, man!" And I'm thinking, Oh shit—I'm sorry, man. It was really funny. After the record, he wrote me a letter thanking me, signed, "The Asshole." [*laughs*]

Did you work the solo out before you cut it?
No, I just noodled along. I actually changed part of the song, though, because they wanted me to solo over the break. So I said, "Can we edit it to a verse, so there's some chord changes?" Then I just soloed over what I thought should be the solo section. I did two solos, and they picked the one they liked. That was it. It took about 20 minutes to do. And there was Michael, standing in the back saying [*mimics Michael Jackson*] "I really like that high fast stuff you do!" [*laughs*]

It seemed logical to assume that as of result of "Beat It" you'd receive a lot of offers to play on other people's records. Yet we haven't seen you do much of that.
Yeah, well, just recently Stevie Nicks...Steve Perg...everybody's calling. Thank God I have an answering machine! [*laughs*] Believe it or not, I did the Michael Jackson thing because I figured nobody'd know. I swear to God. The band—Roth, my brother and Mike—always hated me doing things outside of Van Halen. They'd say, "Keep it in the band." And it just so happened that Roth was on one of his Amazon jungle trips or whatever he does, and Al was out of town, and Mike was out at Disneyland or something, so I couldn't consult them. So I just said, "Damn it, I'll do it and no one will ever know." So then it comes out and becomes song of the year and everything. My brother still won't let me live it down. And I did it for free, too! [*laughs*]

been in the studio before. I remember asking Ted Templeman and Don Landee, "Hey, do you mind if I just play like I do live?" Because I didn't have any rhythm parts underneath the solos. I didn't know how to overdub. That's why it sounds live—it is!

What noticeable changes have you made in the way you now lay down basic tracks?
See, a lot of times I'll still do a live solo, but I'll just overdub the

What about Tone Loc sampling "Jamie's Cryin'"?
[*Excitedly*] Oh, right! I'm sitting around watching MTV one day and I think, That sure sounds like my guitar and Al's drums...

FRANK WHITE

Whether I tap or not, I'm still a good player.

Wait a second. The story I had from the label is that you were consulted.
Hell, no! I was just sitting there, and I hear my brother's drums. And then there's my guitar! So I called up our manager and said, "What is this shit?" So I guess he called them up and said that they should at least thank us. [*laughs*] And I guess we're thanked on the record.

This is done all the time these days. A lot of rap uses hard rock and heavy metal guitar samples.
I think it's a bullshit thing. I mean, why don't they just have someone else play it? It's kinda thin, you know?

Let me ask you about your hearing. Does Pete Townshend's problem cause you any concern?
Well, I'll tell you one thing I don't do, and that's stack my cabinets. Even in the old days, when I used to have the mountainous shit, I only used the bottom cabinets. Just don't stand in front of the stuff. I like to stand in front of them so I can feel my arm hairs move—but not the hair on my head.

You mentioned Satriani and Vai earlier, but did anybody else who came up during the Eighties make you sweat—maybe just a little?
No. See, nobody makes me sweat. If anything, when I hear somebody good, it inspires me, you know? Like when I first heard Holdsworth, that made me want to play! To me, music isn't a competitive thing. There are so many good players around—I'm not in competition with them. I'm not out to be better than anybody. Music is such a personal thing. How can you say someone's better than someone else?

Well, there is some lame stuff out there.
[*laughs*] That's true!

You were pretty involved with Holdsworth's career for a while there.
Yeah, I got him signed to Warner Bros. because I just hated to see this guy who's so amazing selling guitars to stay alive. So I got him signed. I was supposed to co-produce the record with Ted Templeman and Donn Landee. Then—I hate to say this—while we were on tour in South America he just didn't wanna wait like two weeks, you know? So he did it himself...and it ended up being just another Allan Holdsworth record. The guy needs direction, you know what I mean? We did a couple of demos before I went to South America, and one of the songs was great. So he blew it, I think. I really think I could have, well, not necessarily pulled him back, but steered him in a different direction, you know? I was just over my friend Steve Lukather's house, and he played me Allan's new record, and I tell you, I couldn't tell the difference between that and his other records. I don't wanna rag on the guy, because he's an incredible player and he's a good friend. I love him. He just needs direction, that's all.

Have you worked with him since that episode?
Yeah, I talked to him on the phone about a month ago. He called and asked if I'd want to do something with him. And I'd love to, except I don't really have the time right now. When the time is right, sure. It'll be fun. I don't give a damn if it's good or not. Like that thing I did with Brian May; that wasn't good, but it was fun.

I'd sure like to see how Holdsworth does some of his stuff, but I never had the nerve to ask him. It takes me two hands to do what he does with one. I don't know how he pulls it off! I mean, I have a hell of a reach, too, you know? I'd also love to pick Jimmy Page's brain about how he got some of those sounds. It'd be more in terms of sounds than, "How'd you play this?"

How do you feel about Page these days? He's been getting a bad rap.
And that's bullshit. He's a genius. He's a great player, a songwriter and producer, so there you go. Put it this way: he might not be the greatest executor or whatever, but when you hear a Page solo, he speaks. I've always said that Clapton was my main influence, but Page was actually more the way I am, in a reckless abandon kind of way.

Do you still tinker around, building guitars, as you used to?
Not as much as I used to. The only reason I did that was because I was trying to find—well, not necessarily the perfect guitar, but the guitar that served my means. I'll show you... [*Eddie exits, returning momentarily with his famous striped Strat with the Kramer neck.*] It does exactly what I want it to do. I used to build guitars because I wanted one that had a Gibson sound, but with a vibrato bar. I wanted a Strat with a Gibson sound, and that's what this is.

A lot of guitar manufacturers have taken cues from you over the years.
Oh, God, tell me about it.

The non-pickguard. You were about the first to...
The whole vibrato bar, one-pickup thing was my idea. It was actually a mistake, the way I came up with it. I bought a Strat, and took a chisel to it to carve out the rear pickup cavity, the one by the bridge, so I could drop a humbucker into it . But as I removed the pickguard and put the new pickup in, I didn't know how to rewire it—you know, I couldn't get the wires back in. So I thought, Wow, I wonder how it'll work just straight to the volume knob. So I left it like that. Then I made myself a plastic pickguard to cover up the holes, and that's how this concept was born. You know, when I used to play Les Pauls I could never get a good sound out of the front and rear pickups at the same time. If you get a nice fat sound out of the back one and then you put it on the front, it's real muddy. Either that or you have to set it so bright to get a good sound out of the front one that the back pickup sounds like shit. So I just said, "Damn, what do I need two pickups for?"

You don't strike me as a real EQ freak or anything.
Oh, no. I just turn everything up! [*laughs*]

If you turn everything up with some Marshalls, there's either too much treble or too much bass.

EDDIE MALLUK/ATLASICONS.COM

If I had to learn to read music, it would take forever.

Yeah, that's why I use the old ones. Any time I see an old one, I buy it. Even if it sounds like shit, because they can be made to sound good.

Is the Variac still a part of your sound?
Yep.

Does that actually change the voltage?
Yeah, that's all it does.

And you plug the output of the amplifier into the Variac?
Yeah. That's all. It's a light dimmer! I use a studio light dimmer. See, it enables you to play at a lower volume, but you can still get the balls of the amp. I blew out the house once, when we used to live in this little shack in Pasadena. We had this little light dimmer in the wall, and I thought, Wow, I wonder what'll happen if I hook my amp up to that?

What do you think of the guitar sounds we're hearing today? What do you think when you turn on the radio?
I think everybody sounds the same. Playing-wise, too. Everybody has a Marshall stack now, and a guitar like this [*holds up his guitar*] or a Les Paul. Nobody's doing anything different. It all sounds like razor blades coming at your ears after a while. Just fuzzed-out noise.

What if you were a kid today, and there's already an Edward Van Halen out there. What would you do to avoid sounding like a carbon copy?
I don't know...maybe pull out some old Cream records. Listen to old blues stuff and get your feel happening, instead of just jumpin' in and playing as fast as you can, copying the latest hit on the radio. I mean, I don't know what scales are—I just play what sounds right to me. I never had a lesson in my life. So, this scale or that scale, I don't know. To me, you have 12 notes to work with, and whatever configuration you use is up to you.

But didn't you study music theory as a kid?
I was supposed to. It takes too long to learn. I don't even like to read books! If I had to learn to read music, it would take forever.

So a certain amount of ignorance is bliss?
I think the grass is green on both sides—as long as you don't get too caught up in that reading-the-chart syndrome.

What about someone like U2's the Edge, who doesn't have a whole lot of chops but still created an identifiable sound.
He sure likes his echo, doesn't he? But see, there again, he's more of a songwriter, and that's where it's at. Expressing yourself in a song is a lot more wide open then. All these kids who are just gunslingers, they'll come around. You can't be doing that all your life—it's impossible.

Do you ever feel, in a very small way, responsible for the emphasis on speed-playing today?
For kids playing like typewriters? Hey, that's not my fault! Maybe they cop the speed because they can't cop my feel. Maybe they shouldn't think so much. I don't think when I play. I get the basic parts of the song and then, when I start soloing, I don't think.

While we're on the subject of sound, "Finish What Ya Started" is kind of a departure for you.
It's a direct Strat. It was just for fun. We actually set out and tried to do something different, something goofy, and it worked.

Is it too early to talk about what you might do on the next Van Halen record?
Oooh. [*pauses*] Anything and everything. Sammy and I are already writing, and we're comin' up with some really neat shit.

Is there any format you follow when you write together?
Uh, I come up with music, he calls me and comes up with a concept, an idea—God, I don't wanna give anything away here—and he'll inspire me to write something. And then when I do, I'll inspire him, in turn, to write the lyrics to it. And then we sit down together and work it out. Then Al and Mike jump in and say, "We don't like that!" [*laughs*] No, I'm kidding. We never really write in the studio. The studio's just where we go to record. I just sit around with my guitar and a little cassette machine.

We've never had the luxury to do what we're doing right now, and that is stockpiling a bunch of tunes and then when we're ready to put it out, putting it out. Because with *5150*, you know, everybody was wondering what was going on with Van Halen, so we released it. And with *OU812*, we were already committed to do the Monsters of Rock tour [*with Scorpions, Metallica, Dokken and Kingdom Come*] before the record was even done. We would have preferred to finish the record, put it out, waited a bit, made sure we liked the record, and then booked a tour. That's what we're going to do this time.

How do you feel today about the Monsters of Rock tour?
A lot of people slammed us for it, but we sold a lot of tickets. Not all of them were sold out, but hey, they were stadiums. That same year, Aerosmith and Guns N' Roses did the same thing, and they only sold like 30,000 seats outdoors. I didn't hear anybody raggin' about that.

You received so much flak about playing keyboards. Do you think people still don't see you as a keyboard player?
I love playing keyboards, man. I write a lot of stuff on keys. It's like they don't want to realize that I play keyboards. See, here's the thing: when Dave was in the band, he would say, "Hey, man, nobody wants to see you play keyboards!" And I felt like, "If I wanna play keyboards or if I wanna play tuba, I'll play it."

Let's look ahead 10 years. Do you see yourself doing the same thing, with the same band?
Oh, yeah. Definitely. I'm totally into family, so to speak. There's no reason why I can't be doing the same thing. I just want to make music and have fun. As long as you have the fire and you still want to do it, fine. When it starts getting old to me, then I'll start doing something else. I don't know what—maybe a race car driver! ✉

Reprinted from Guitar World, *February 1995*

CUT AND DRY

Edward Van Halen Trims his hair, quits drinking and regains his *Balance.*

- - - - -

by Tom Beaujour with Greg Di Benedetto

EDWARD VAN HALEN welcomes me to 5150, his legendary 24-track home studio, with a handshake and a slap on the back. But for a split second I am unable to return the warm greeting, as I am dumbstruck: standing in front of me, it seems, is not Edward, but his evil twin. // The guitarists moppish hair has been lopped off, leaving in its place an expertly styled flattop. Van Halen's soft-featured face, once frozen into a perpetually boyish grin, has been hardened by a newly sprouted goatee. When I gather the courage to ask what prompted this drastic makeover, Edward's response is amiable.

"I lost a golf bet with [*Buffalo Bills quarterback*] Jim Kelly, and ended up having to shave my head with a fucking Norelco razor," he explains. "I just decided to leave it short, because I was sick of having long hair."

The fact is, Edward is a changed man in far more significant ways than his choice of 'do. For the most part, the guitarist has abandoned the pyrotechnic guitar antics that rocketed him to prominence 17 years ago, opting instead for a more lyrical, restrained approach to his instrument. More significantly, Edward, who will turn 40 in January, is the father of a three-and-a-half-year-old son, Wolfgang, and he takes his role as a parent extremely seriously. Unlike many celeb-

rities whose involvement with their children extends only to child-support payments, Edward lovingly subjects himself to the unglamorous but rewarding rigors of everyday parenting. "Wolfie wakes us up at six in the morning, saying, 'Come on, you're mine, Daddy. I want to do this. I want to do that,' " he says with a doting smile. "I take him to school every morning."

No sooner have I dispensed with the pre-interview pleasantries when Edward whisks me into the studio's control room. As he prepares to crank up the band's soon-to-be-released album, *Balance*, on the studio's ear-annihilating monitors, Van Halen pauses, his finger poised on the CD player's "play" button.

ROBERT KNIGHT ARCHIVE/REDFERNS/GETTY IMAGES

"You know," he says with a concerned look, "you should proba-bly listen to this in the car because it sounds much better in there. We mastered this record differently than the last one, and it sounds more ballsy—except in here."

Tempted as I am by the offer to hang out in one of Edward's many fine automobiles, I politely decline, opting to remain in the more spacious and well-lit environment of the control room. "Well, okay," says Eddie. "Here we go!"

The album opens with an ominous Tibetan monk chant sample which gives way to the lush, heavy layers of "Seventh Seal." Suddenly the music stops. "You have to listen to this in the car," says Edward. "It really sounds better."

Moments later, the two of us are seated in what must be the Van Halens' new family car, a charcoal-gray Mercedes sedan. In spite of the vehicle's austere looks, the stereo system is brutally loud, and *Balance*'s wave of guitar goodness swallows us alive. Edward sits qui-

etly, his eyes closed as he basks in the glory of his own creation. Periodically, he wakes from his deep-listening trance to point out a particularly noteworthy lick or explain the origin of a song. Apparently, Van Halen's success has not lessened the mixture of excitement and apprehension that he, like most musicians, feels when unveiling a just-completed piece of work.

Consistent with Edward's new-found maturity are his most recent efforts to put an end to his well-documented drinking habit. "I think that God gave me one big bottle of alcohol and I drank it real fast," he says. "God gives everyone a bottle when they're born, and they have to make it last a lifetime. Well, I drank mine too quickly, so I just can't drink anymore."

Surprisingly, Edward, who will consume several non-alcoholic beers during the course of the interview, is more than willing to discuss the topic of his drinking at great length.

Although it may come as a shock to some, hard rock's perennial

ROBERT KNIGHT ARCHIVE/REDFERNS/GETTY IMAGES

completed *Balance* more quickly than any other album we've done in years. We wrote, recorded and mastered the whole fucking thing in five months. We started in June, and by the end of October it was mastered.

What kind of pre-production work did you do to prepare for the recording of *Balance*?
We demoed about 20 songs for Bruce. Actually, we over-cut! There are like four songs that aren't even on the record. It just got too long. We had an hour's worth of music in the can, and Bruce said, "Do you want to do a double CD or what?"

How did you decide which songs should go on the record?
Well, out of, say, 20 songs, the ones that got finished first ended up on the record.

Sometimes, when I focus on writing, I start blazing: I'll come up with all kinds of shit and it overwhelms Sammy for a bit. The way he works best is when he focuses on one thing and writes lyrics for it. So, since I was writing so much, a lot of lyrics weren't done. For example, for the instrumental track, "Baluchitherium," we were actually working on lyrics and we ended up going, "Fuck it, it sounds pretty good without vocals," so we left it. And Sammy was relieved— "Okay, I got one less to work on." So, yeah, there are actually four more tunes that the music is finished for. We'll finish those for the next record, or whenever.

Even though you made the album so quickly, the song arrangements seem more thoughtfully developed than anything you've done in the past.
Yeah, they are. Bruce just said, "Work, motherfuckers." He's a serious guy. He walks in with his briefcase and says, "This is what we're doing today." We would be like, "Oh fuck, I don't want to do it. Let's do that tomorrow." He always answered, "No, you're doing it now." [*laughs*] It was great working with him. We're doing the next record with him, too.

He's a very musical guy. He dabbles in a little bit of everything, plays a little guitar and a little piano, but his main instrument is trumpet. He's producing Chicago right now—a big band horn thing. Bruce isn't like certain producers who spend all their time on the phone and every once in a while ask, "Got it yet?" He's a hands-on guy.

Were you at all worried that Bruce, who produced Aerosmith's last couple of albums, might make the band sound too slick?
No. A good producer brings out the best in the artist he's working with. You shouldn't be able to listen to something and say, "So-and-so produced this album." Bruce's stamp is not on our record because a good producer should not have a stamp. People who are only capable of molding a band to fit their "trademark" sound are bullshit producers. Bruce, on the other hand, just enhanced the best parts of what the band already had to offer.

Van Halen recording sessions have in the past been fueled by large quantities of alcohol, but drunkenness and dissipation don't seem to be compatible with Bruce's disciplinarian production style. I notice that right now, at least, you're drinking a non-alcoholic beer. Are you not drinking at all anymore?
No, I'm not.

How long has it been since you stopped?
It's been off and on. This time about a month. Actually, I did really well while we made the record. I played a lot of stuff sober, which really weirded me out. It took me a while to get into it without the help of the alcohol.

What is it about drinking that facilitates your playing?
There's like this wall, and when I drink, my inhibitions are lower so I just wing stuff without getting embarrassed or nervous. But I have to

whiz kid has become a man.

Was all of the new album recorded here at 5150?
Almost everything was done here, except for five lead vocal tracks, which were recorded in Vancouver.

Why did you go there?
Because Bruce Fairbairn, our producer, lives up there. He would fly down every Monday morning and we'd work during the week. On the weekends, he'd go home. We had promised him before we began recording that we'd do some vocals up there so that he could be with his family a little more.

It seems awfully adult for Van Halen to be sticking to the kind of rigid recording schedule you're describing.
Bruce is very structured. He wouldn't let us loaf for a minute, so we

God gave me one big bottle of alcohol
and I drank it real fast.

get past that because drinking's no good. I've been doing it too long.

Do you have any insight into why you've had so much trouble stopping?
Because I can't stop! I'm an alcoholic. It's like, "Just a couple? Fuck you! I'll drink until I go to sleep."

Your father had a drinking problem as well, didn't he?
Yes, but I think my problem is more a product of my environment than any genetic factor. I remember my dad got me drinking and smoking when I was 12. I was nervous, so he said to me, "Here. Have a shot of vodka." Boom—I wasn't nervous anymore. My mom used to buy me cigarettes and it just stuck, it was habit. I don't drink for the taste of it, I drink to get a fucking buzz. I like to get drunk. I really do.

Do you think that the fact that your work schedule is less rigid than most people's has resulted in your drinking more?
You know, believe it or not, I drink more when I'm playing and writing and working than when I'm not. I come up to the studio and drink and work. When I go into the house, I don't drink. If I spend a weekend at the beach, I don't drink. So it's really funny.

It's definitely uncommon.
For me, leisure time is not the problem area. My problem is that I go to the office to drink. It's completely ass-backward. And the only reason I keep doing it is because it still works, believe it or not. It just breaks down the inhibitions. And I'm too inhibited, ordinarily—I get real nervous.

You said you recorded most of *Balance* sober.
Yeah, but sometimes, I would listen back to something and go, "Ooh, that's stiff. Let me redo that."

Uh-oh.
But I didn't drink too much. When we made the last record, I had at least 12 to 15 beers in me each day. This time, nobody but me drank while we were working. And if I got a little bit overboard, I'd say "I'm out of here, I'm too far gone," and call it a day.

Do you know what I've noticed that's funny? When I'm really tired, I feel the same as when I'm drunk, because it's easier for me to get through to the other side, or whatever you want to call it. It's easier for me to just let go and not judge what I'm doing. It's all about just opening up and being free. But if I'm drinking I don't even think about it. It's like, "Oh, I made a mistake, big fucking deal."

Overall, *Balance* seems to be a darker record than *For Unlawful Carnal Knowledge* and its immediate predecessors. What inspired you to write the music?
I don't really know what inspires me to write the music I do, but usu-

ally, the music will set the tone for the lyrics. I don't think it's really that dark. The first tune, "Seventh Seal," is kind of that way, but "Can't Stop Loving You" is an awesome rock groove.

There are more songs written in minor keys than on the last record.
D minor. Everything's in D minor, the saddest of all keys.

While we were listening to the record a little while ago, you indicated that you recorded the strange piano piece, "Strung Out," back in the early Eighties.
Yeah, I forget exactly what year that was, but it was before '84. Valerie [*Bertinelli, Edward's wife*] and I had rented [*popular composer, pianist and arranger*] Marvin Hamlisch's beach house for the summer. I just used to waste this beautiful piano. It was like a Baldwin or a Yamaha. It had cigarette burns all over it and I was sticking everything but the kitchen sink in it: ping-pong balls, D batteries, knives, forks—I even broke a few strings.

I don't know what prompted me to do it. I was just fucking around. Actually, it started off with me playing the strings with my fingers. I would create harmonics by hitting the key and muffling the string up and down to bring harmonics out like on a guitar. I have like 10 tapes of this stuff, and Bruce picked out this little part. He loved it.

Was Hamlisch furious when he returned to his house?
Yeah, he was. I tried to get the piano fixed before he came back, but he found out somehow. I guess they didn't repaint it as well as they could have.

You feature an acoustic guitar very prominently on "Take Me Back," one of the tracks off the new album. What finally prompted you to go "unplugged," if only for a moment?
I actually wrote that ditty a while ago. I wanted to put it on the last record, but we never really completed it. This time around I really wanted to finish the song, because I still really liked it. So we worked it up.

What kind of acoustic did you use?
It's a South American guitar called a Musser. I bought it at [*L.A. vintage shop*] Norm's Rare Guitars.

Other than using an acoustic, did you do anything else out of the ordinary for the album?
Nope. As usual, I have two Shure SM-57s miking one cabinet. Pretty much everything was recorded with the 5150 amp, but I did use the old Marshall Super Lead head on about three tunes. The stuff that's real clean-sounding, like "Aftershock," was done with the Marshall.

Why did you decide to use the Marshall again?
Just to get a different sound.

Hagar (right) and Van Halen onstage at the Shoreline Amphitheater in Mountain View, CA, on August 20, 1995.

TIM MOSENFELDER/GETTY IMAGES

Even though this record has a drier sound than *For Unlawful Carnal Knowledge*, the guitars still have that chorus-y shimmer that's become a staple of your sound lately. Do you double most of your rhythm tracks?

No, not at all. But everything has the Eventide harmonizer on it. The dry guitar signal is on the left, and the duplicate sound that the Eventide generates is on the right. I barely use the harmonizer as an effect; it's just to split my guitar to both sides of the stereo spectrum. I have it set to detune to 98, so it harmonizes just a little.

When did you start splitting your signal like this?

I think *Fair Warning*, or the album after. Maybe *5150*. I forget. But that's been my thing ever since.

In the old days, Donn Landee [*engineer on every Van Halen album from 1978's* Van Halen *through 1988's* OU812] would have my dry signal on the left and a little echo or reverb on the right. And I'm going, "Well, why don't we use the harmonizer and get the whole fucking guitar over there instead of just [*makes breathy noise to imitate the decay of a reverb or Echoplex unit*] the tail-end of everything I play. I hated that sound.

Really? I always thought of it as a really cool trademark of your sound.

I can't stand it. I guess it worked for the first record. But after that it got old really fast. If you have a car and the left speaker's blown, the guitar is gone. If you're sitting on the right in the back seat, you don't hear the guitar even if both front speakers work. What kind of shit is that?

It sounds like you have your guitar plugged into a Leslie on "Not Enough."

We plugged the Marshall into the Leslie via this preamp box that my tech, Matt Bruck, brought over. He had used it on the demo tape for his band, Zen Boy. He hooked me up and I just played it.

What inspired the solo on that song?

I was hearing a Beatles-ish feel, so I went for a "While My Guitar Gently Weeps" kind of thing.

The songs on *Balance* seem to have more key changes than your previous work.

It's called "better songwriting." [*laughs*]

Has your piano training given you an increased understanding of harmony, which in turn helps your songwriting?

Yeah, totally.

You play some barrelhouse piano on "Big Fat Money," but besides that, there aren't very many keyboards on *Balance.* Is there a reason for that?

Yeah, I haven't really spent that much time playing piano lately. I think that old synth sound didn't feel right for this record. I might use it in the future, though. Who knows.

"Big Fat Money" has an unusual solo that's almost humorous. What prompted that radical departure from your usual style?

That was Bruce's idea. He's going, "Hey, let's go for a jazz sound." And I'm going, "Okay." So I pulled out an old 335, ran it through my Marshall set really low and just did it. It's funny.

At the end of the instrumental track "Baluchitherium," there's an entire menagerie of guitar sounds.

That's exactly what it is. It sounds like a bunch of animals—like a zoo. There's a bunch of birds and chirps and dinosaur calls and the elephant sounds I've always made. It just felt like a fun thing to do. You can even hear my dog Sherman howling on there.

What mic did you use on the dog?

Uhhh, a Sennheiser. [*laughs*] We have pictures of it too; it's so funny. We had to tape a hot dog to the microphone. Swear to God. The dog was afraid of the mic. We kept pushing him up there and he'd back off. So we taped the hot dog to it, and then started making a bunch of noise.

wouldn't do all the loony gymnastic shit. What's the point? That stuff goes in one ear and out the other.

It appeals to a select group of people.

Yeah, I mean, who can play the fastest, who can do this, who can do that. Fuck, who cares? I stopped doing that years ago. On this album, I focused on fitting the song. For example, on "Take Me Back" I did a little slide ditty that just fit the song, instead of playing an actual solo. "Seventh Seal" has no solo at all. Instead, I added a musical interlude that worked for the song.

On *Van Halen*, I was a young punk, and everything revolved around the fastest kid in town—the gunslinger attitude. But I'd say that at the time of *Fair Warning*, I started concentrating more on songwriting. But I guess in most people's minds I'm just a gunslinger. The thing is, I do so much more than just blow fucking solos. Actually, that's the least of what I do.

To what extent do you think the success of Van Halen still rests upon your skills as a guitar player?

I have no idea. I don't analyze it. I try to concentrate on writing good songs and, hopefully, people will like them.

Have you ever considered leaving your unaccompanied solo out of your live shows?

I've thought about it many times. Actually, back when Sammy joined

> # I enjoy what I do—creating something as opposed to making a part for an Impala or something.

We actually bought a tape of a fire engine. We'd play the tape, and Sherman would get up to the mic, sniff the hot dog, and bark.

In addition to the dog and the other animals, it also sounded like there was some six-string bass on that song.

Actually, no. You know what I used? It was a Music Man Albert Lee model guitar that I strung with heavier strings and tuned down to low A.

What does "Baluchitherium" mean?

Actually, Valerie tipped me to it. When she heard the song for the first time, she said, "That sounds like a dinosaur song," because it sounds so big. She started looking through a book and said, "How about 'baluchitherium?' " And I'm going, "What the fuck is that?" I started reading, and it turns out that the baluchitherium was the biggest mammal that lived in the prehistoric age. Valerie always titles songs. She titled "1984."

It's surprising you don't really solo over the track, since there are no vocals in the way.

I just wanted a simple melodic feel. Even if there were to be a solo, it would only diverge from the melody a little bit. A lot of times, if there's a melody there, I prefer to stick to it, or maybe play with it a little, as opposed to indulging in gymnastics.

It comes back to the same old question people are always asking me: "When are you going to do a solo record?" Well, if I did, it would probably be similar to "Baluchitherium," meaning it would be Van Halen music—which I write anyway—but without singing. I

the band, I said, "I'm tired of doing fucking guitar solos," but everyone insisted that I had to keep doing them.

Isn't it still a thrill for you to have people focusing on you alone and to hear them scream your name?

Yeah, but it's such masturbation. A lot of it is just screaming, "Look at me!" Some parts of the solo, like "Cathedral" or "Eruption," are little compositions, and I don't mind doing those. But, still, what's the point? I get bored doing it.

In one of your previous *Guitar World* interviews, you said that sometimes you're a little embarrassed that you popularized the two-handed tapping technique, because it became such an overused gimmick.

I did feel that way, but I don't anymore, because nobody's tapping these days.

Even you don't tap as much as you once did.

I do it as much as I always have. It's part of my playing. I used it all over the record; you just can't tell. I probably tap a little bit in every song. To me it's a part of my playing, it's not, "Oh, I'm going to do my trick now."

Were you criticized for "selling out" when you let Pepsi use "Right Now" for their ill-fated Crystal Pepsi advertising campaign?

Probably, but the only reason we gave them the music was because they were going to use the song anyway. They would just have recut

EDDIE MALLUK/ATLASICONS.COM

the song with studio musicians, like they do for some TV movies when they redo an old hit because they can't use the original. If they use the original, they've got to pay, but if they don't, all they do is give credit to the artist and then pay the studio cats. Pepsi told us that they were going to do that, so we said, "Hey wait a minute, we might as well get the money." I ain't that proud, you know. I'm not going to say—"No, go ahead, rip us off. And keep the money too!"

What's a day in the life of Edward Van Halen like?

I spend time with my son, Wolfie, and play a bit of golf. Actually, I started to take some lessons last week, because I'm still a hack at it. I don't get out there enough. It's a cool game for life, because when I'm fucking 90, I could still be doing it, so I might as well learn how to play now.

Our whole road crew plays, so on the road, you get to hang with the guys—which is an awful lot of fun. Golf isn't really about hitting the ball, it's more about male bonding. Letting it hang.

Does your son, who you seem to spend much of your time with, play an instrument yet?

He likes to beat on Al's drums and he loves piano. The other day, actually, Valerie and I were up above the garage where I keep all of my guitars, looking for something, and Wolfie saw all the guitars and said—he was so decisive—"You know, when I get bigger, I'm going to play the guitar." [*laughs*] It's like, "Okay, take your pick." He said it with such conviction!

Actually, he isn't exposed to that much music because I really don't play in the house. You figure that he'd be doused with music from the minute he wakes up until he goes to bed at night, but no. He has a normal kid life: he watches Barney and Mickey Mouse and all that shit.

So you try and make sure that Wolfie leads a normal life?

No, it's just that I'm normal. I don't do anything that out of the ordinary. He hates loud noise so he'll come in here and go, "Daddy, too loud. Too loud!" Yeah, he makes me turn the shit way down. It's really funny.

He knows that you play music, but do you think he understands your "unique" situation?

I don't think so. I don't think he's got that yet. Sometimes, I'll say, "I'm going to work now, Wolfie," and he answers, "You mean you go to the studio?" Then he comes here to visit me when I'm trying to write, and I'll be sitting here with my thumb up my ass, smoking cigarettes and plinking around on the guitar. To him, that's what Daddy does for work. He'll put it together later, I guess, but right now he probably sees other people going to work whereas I just take the golf cart up here.

What's the best thing about being Edward Van Halen?

It's a great feeling for people to like what you do. I do what I like and other people like it. It's a great payoff. How many people get to experience that?

The other day, I was playing golf on a public course in Pasadena with these two old timers, and one guy says, "Shit, man, a bad day on the course is better than any good day at work." And I started thinking, Well, I guess for you, but I like my work. I'm really lucky, because I really enjoy making music. I don't consider it to be like clocking in and doing a job.

I'm not making light of making music either. It's hard work, but I enjoy what I do—creating something as opposed to making a part for an Impala or something. I'm just lucky to have found that. And that's half of it: me enjoying what I do. The other half is when other people dig it. That's like, "Whoo! Home run!" ▄

Reprinted from Guitar World, *April 2008*

LIKE FATHER, LIKE SON

Eddie Van Halen put the fire in the group that bears his name. It took his son, Wolfgang, to rekindle the passion and get the group on the road for one of the most anticipated reunion tours in rock history. In this world exclusive interview, the father-and-son duo talk about their relationship, working and performing together, and the rebirth of Van Halen.

- - - - -

by Chris Gill

S MUSICAL TALENT genetically inherited? If your test sample is the Van Halen family, the answer undoubtedly would be yes and the proof would be the current Van Halen tour, which features the Van Halen brothers—Alex and Ed—on drums and guitar respectively, as well as Ed's 16-year-old son Wolfgang on bass. Although Wolfgang picked up the bass less than two years ago, his comfort on arena stages in front of crowds of 20,000 fans suggests that it was always in his DNA to be a performer.

KEVIN MAZUR/WIREIMAGE/GETTY IMAGES

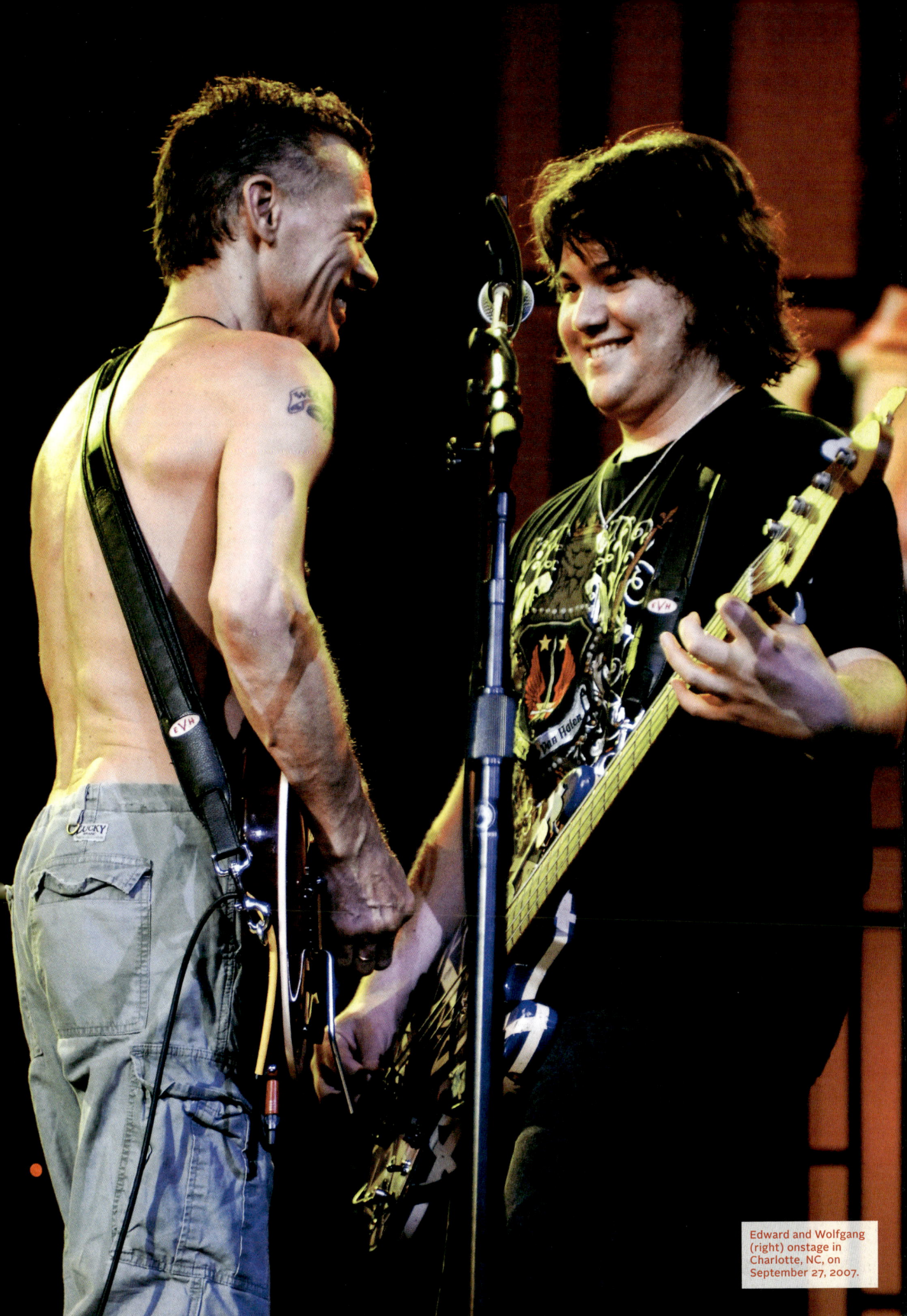

Edward and Wolfgang (right) onstage in Charlotte, NC, on September 27, 2007.

I couldn't wait for the day I'd be able to make music with my son.

Wolfgang's membership in the band may now seem like pre-determined fate, but Ed was careful from the beginning to let Wolfgang's musical interests and talents develop naturally, even though Ed often hinted that he hoped his kid would follow in his footsteps. "I'm going to let Wolfgang be whatever he wants to be," he stated in 1995 when Wolfgang was only four. "I don't see how he won't somehow be into music, being exposed to it all the time. But I'm not going to force him to play piano or take music lessons like my parents did to me."

Wolfgang's guest appearances on guitar during Van Halen's 2004 tour showed that Ed's kid had not only taken an interest in music but he had also quickly developed true talent as a musician. Even so, devoted fans were taken by complete surprise when Ed revealed in late 2006 that Wolfgang was Van Halen's new bass player. A few months later when news leaked that David Lee Roth was returning as the band's vocalist and a tour was in the works, critics wondered if Wolfgang was truly qualified. Playing one of the most anticipated tours of the past 20 years is a hell of a first job for anyone, let alone someone who was just 16 years old and never played in any other bands before.

What seemed like a risky move on paper proved instead to be an overwhelming success as Wolfgang breathed new life into the band with the right balance of youthful enthusiasm and devoted reverence to the band's classic songs, all of which were recorded several years before Wolfgang was even born. While the tour gives Van Halen fans an opportunity to see the band with David Lee Roth again, the presence of Wolfgang onstage opens the door to a new chapter in the band's history. What lies ahead in the future is anyone's guess, but with Wolfgang joining the band its foundation is now stronger than ever as is its potential to grow in new directions.

Talking with Ed and Wolfgang, several unusual qualities become evident. There's no generation gap between the two, but more importantly they reveal an undeniable mutual respect and admiration for each other that even Wolfgang's occasional rebelliousness and Ed's playful displays of parental authority can't hide. The two are truly in awe of each other's talents. One gets the feeling that Wolfgang would be a huge Van Halen fan even if his dad wasn't in the band and that Ed would want to make music with Wolfgang even if Wolfgang wasn't his son.

With rave reviews coming in for the band's current tour and a lifetime of possibilities lying ahead to explore, the future for Van Halen as a band looks very bright thanks to the addition of a new family member. As the saying goes, the family that plays together stays together, and this family positively jams.

How did Wolfgang join the band? Did you ask him to join?

EDDIE VAN HALEN I asked him. We were in the studio one day, just jamming on some stuff.

WOLFGANG VAN HALEN Actually there's a story behind that. It was in the summer of '06. My dad said, "Hey, do you want to jam?" and I said, "Sure."

ED I'll never forget it. [*to Wolfgang*] You played the blonde five-string bass with four strings on it.

KEVIN WINTER/GETTY IMAGES (LEFT); THEO WARGO/GETTY IMAGES (MIDDLE); SCOTT LEGATO/ATLASICONS.COM (RIGHT)

WOLFGANG Oh yeah!

ED It was the first time that he played bass.

So, the drum room is in the back of the studio. Al was in there, and he couldn't see us, and we couldn't see him. Wolfgang picked up the bass and I put the bass in Al's headphones. It was the first time in 30 years that Al's had bass in his headphones. Al said, "Hey! How are you playing bass and guitar at the same time?" I got on the talkback and said, "Say hi, Wolfie!" and you went [*in high voice*], "Hi, Uncle Al!" Your voice was a lot higher then. Al went, "Who's playing bass?" I told him it was Wolfie, and it blew Al's mind.

WOLFGANG After that, Al asked if I wanted to jam again. I said, "Yeah!"

ED That's when I asked him if he'd like to be the bass player in Van Halen. He said, "Yeah, as long as I don't have to do a certain thing," which I won't mention. [*laughs deviously*]

WOLFGANG I can say that: I said, "Sure. I just don't want to do a bass solo."

So in the beginning everything happened organically.

WOLFGANG We didn't lay out a plan or anything. It just fell together. We played together a good four months without any vocals, and we just looked at each other and knew it was awesome.

ED It's like Dave says, "Three parts original, one part inevitable." And it was inevitable.

Wolfgang, you play several instruments—guitar, drums, keyboards. What drove you toward the bass?

WOLFGANG Well, it was the only open spot. [*everyone laughs*] And the people filling the other spots—drums and guitar—are the two greatest players of those instruments in the frickin' world. I find the bass safe. You don't have to go out on the line.

ED I remember another thing you said at the very beginning: "Can I just groove?"

WOLFGANG I just like to be there to groove and keep the song going.

Was the time in between when the tour was announced and when you played the first show difficult?

WOLFGANG I just wanted to get it over with. I wanted to be where we are now. There was so much weight on my shoulders to fill the shoes and prove that I could do it. I *knew* I could do it, but I wanted to say, "Everybody, hey, I *can* do it!"

ED We rehearsed probably six months before Dave showed up. We were almost over-rehearsed. We got to the point where we were goofing around.

WOLFGANG That's when we started playing "Little Dreamer" in double time.

ED When Dave walked in it blew his freakin' mind.

WOLFGANG That night was magical. That was the first time I heard vocals with everything.

ED Dave couldn't believe how good you are.

Wolf you've gone directly from rehearsing with your dad and uncle to playing some of the biggest venues in the world. Was it difficult for you to make that transition?

WOLFGANG Because we rehearsed so frickin' much, from spending six months in 5150, then at Center Staging and then for a few weeks at the L.A. Forum, I felt that we had done enough preparation for me to feel safe. Plus when you're on the stage. you're far enough away from people that you feel comfortable. With the lights and everything sometimes I can just close my eyes and feel like we're in that room at 5150 again.

ED It's a lot different than rehearsing in the studio. It's probably more comfortable than being in the control room with a bunch of people staring at you.

WOLFGANG It's definitely a lot more open. That room is claustrophobic.

ED I've always said that the more people there are, the more chance there is that someone will like it.

WOLFGANG When there are only 10 people around, I get nervous. But when there are so many other people I feel more comfortable. Then it's just the four of us doing our thing.

ED If there's just one person and they don't like you, you're fucked. If you've got two people at least, there's a 50-50 chance that at least one of the two people will like you, hopefully.

Van Halen performing in Louisville, KY, on February 18, 2012.

How did your dad help you prepare for the tour?

ED The first thing I told him is look out for the bitches!

Wolfgang performing for friends and family at a dress rehearsal in Inglewood, CA, February 8, 2012.

KEVIN WINTER/GETTY IMAGES

WOLFGANG He didn't really help me prepare. He just told me what not to do.

ED I taught him what my dad taught me, which is you can learn from everyone.

WOLFGANG That, and practice.

ED Actually he helped me more than I helped him.

WOLFGANG Yeah, I had to teach him how to play the songs again.

ED Because I couldn't remember the damn songs, and I don't know how to work a fuckin' iPod. He had one with all the songs on it. We hooked it up in the control room, and he'd go, "No dad, it goes like this!"

Did you teach yourself how to play the songs?

WOLFGANG Yeah, I did. The night before we started practicing, I sat down in my music room and l listened to every single song and just played to them. I didn't do exactly everything that's on the recordings. I put my own spin on it, but not enough to make people go, "Whoa, what's wrong with the bass?" I kept it as close as possible but added just a little...*spice*. A little WVH flair. [*laughs*]

Ed, What's it like to be onstage with your son as a band member, not just a special guest like he was on the previous tour?

ED It's an amazing feeling. I'm just so truly blessed. I have pictures of me sitting in the racquetball court in my pajamas with an acoustic guitar and Wolfgang is probably just two-and-a-half-feet tall. I'll never forget the day I saw his foot tapping along in beat! I knew then, I couldn't wait for the day I'd be able to make music with my son. I don't know what more I could ask for.

Even after playing about 40 shows together, do you still have moments?

ED Oh yeah. Every night. Sometimes we actually talk while we're playing. I'll go, "Hey! Are you all right?" because sometimes he'll look at me funny. When I give him a kiss or a high five or a low five, it's from the heart. It ain't bullshit. It's just pure love.

WOLFGANG That doesn't happen to me every night, but sometimes when I'm playing I'll forget to sing or play a certain note I'll look up and go, "Whoa, this is crazy!" That feeling is always there, but I don't always have time to think about it because I have a job to do.

What's it like to be in a band with your dad and uncle?

WOLFGANG It feels right.

ED That's the perfect way to put it. It just feels right.

WOLFGANG I don't ever go, "This is weird. I'm with a bunch of older people." I feel like we're all the same age. It's just what we do.

ED I was going to say the same thing. Every now and then when we're onstage playing, I'll look at him and go, God, that's my son! He's only 16, but he's not 16. He's an equal. Age doesn't matter.

WOLFGANG There's nobody else my age on the tour, but I feel like I'm an equal. I hope that everybody thinks of me the same way.

ED I believe they do, but you wouldn't believe the legalities we had to go through to have him be the bass player in Van Halen.

WOLFGANG I still have school.

How are your friends reacting to your first job?

WOLFGANG My friends just see me as me. It's Wolfie. He's doing his thing.

ED But they must trip.

WOLFGANG They do. But they all really support me.

ED I'm sure they're proud of you.

What music do you listen to?

WOLFGANG Mainly rock stuff. Nothing too out of the ordinary. I really like Tool, which is one of my favorite bands, and I love Primus and Sevendust, too.

ED You were totally into AC/DC for a while.

WOLFGANG AC/DC is in all of our hearts because they rule.

ED You listen to us, too.

WOLFGANG Not any more. I haven't listened to us for a while.

ED That's because you're playing it now. I remember when I picked you up from school one day and there were boxes of records sitting in the shop at the studio. You looked at them and went, "Is this all you, dad?"

WOLFGANG Oh yeah. I probably was like five.

ED No, I think you were 10.

WOLFGANG Whatever.

ED It blew my mind that I totally forgot to turn him on to all the music that I've written. All he knew was what he heard on the radio.

WOLFGANG Like "Jump," and that was it.

ED I'll never forget when we were coming home from Castle Park [*a family entertainment center*]. "Hot for Teacher" came on the radio and Wolf was going, "Who is that singing?" I said, "That's Dave."

You write a lot of material. Do you have a gauge in your head that lets you know when something is ready to serve up to the table?

ED There's a lot of stuff I like that the rest of the guys don't. It's like that with "Panama." I rarely start on the one, and Al hears what I'm playing backward. I'll never forget when I wrote "Little Dreamer," which is one of the few where I do start on the one and he played backward to that too. Onstage when we're playing...

WOLFGANG ...Oh God, I have to watch you! At the end of "Unchained" we have to go eight or nine times before we freakin' end! Sometimes it's three. Sometimes it's five. It's always an odd number.

ED I can't count for some reason. It's always threes or fives for some reason. I only go by feel.

WOLFGANG And sometimes that feeling is wrong! [*laughs*] But we always somehow manage to pull it together for the ending.

ED We fall down the stairs and land on our feet together. Onstage, I look at Wolfie because he can count!

Has it always been that way, even before Wolfgang?

ED Yeah! But now I've got two people to help me, because both Al and Wolfie can count.

How do you approach your solo section every night?

ED There are certain things that I feel the fans really want to hear me play. "Eruption." "Cathedral."

WOLFGANG "Spanish Fly." The "Little Guitars" intro.

ED I noodle a bit. About the only complaint I get is that my solo is too long. Half the time I'm looking over at [*guitar tech*] Matt Bruck and going, Shit! Where do I go from here? Sometimes I don't know where to go because I forget all of the stuff that I've done. It's like what you asked me about why Van Halen's music has held up. It's because it's spontaneous and real. I'm not saying there's no thought behind it. Obviously it has to have some kind of structure. But spontaneity is the main ingredient.

Wolfgang, do you eventually see yourself having a solo segment onstage?

WOLFGANG I don't. I like having just my own moment for five seconds, like the "So This Is Love?" intro and doing the tapping part in "Romeo Delight." That's enough for me. It's like, Hey! Watch me play! I can do it! I'm more than fulfilled by being a team player.

What was your best personal moment so far on this tour?

WOLFGANG When we did the rehearsal show for our friends and family in L.A. It was just the beginning and I didn't feel I had ripened yet. When we came back to L.A. and did the first Staples Center show, I felt a sense of accomplishment. I was much a better player. I felt like a member of the band.

ED For me it's the fact that I get to play with my son, my brother and Dave. Every night is special. Doing an interview with my son right now is special. It's all special. ◼

UNCHAINED MELODIES

Eddie reflects on some of Van Halen's greatest hits.

- - - - -

by Steven Rosen

Reprinted from Guitar World, *January 1997*

"I'M not saying every song is a Top 40 hit, but they're all tunes that people want to hear when we play live," says Eddie Van Halen, describing the criteria he used to choose the songs that appear on Van Halen's *Best of Volume 1.*

Eddie seems genuinely happy to be talking about his music. In fact, he seems to be happy to talk about anything other than Van Halen's recent lead singer crisis. For the uninitiated, Sammy Hagar is out, David Lee Roth is out, and ex-Extreme frontman Gary Cherone has officially been declared Van Halen's new lead vocalist.

Unfortunately, with all the wild speculation over the future of Van Halen, the true purpose of *Best of Volume 1*—to celebrate the band's brilliant past—has been obscured. To right this wrong, we asked Sir Edward, the guitar hero's guitar hero, to focus his sharp eye and dry wit on the 17 tracks featured on the first Van Halen retrospective ever.

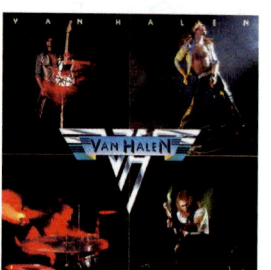

Let's begin with what is perhaps rock's most famous guitar solo, "Eruption."
That was originally just a guitar solo I performed regularly in our club days. When we were recording our first album, our producer, Ted Templeman, heard me practicing it for an upcoming gig and asked, "What the hell is that?" I said, "It's a thing I do live—it's my guitar solo." His immediate reaction was, "Shit, roll tape!" And I

said, "Whatever you say, Mr. Templeman."

We did it twice and that was it. Actually, when I get up high on the neck I make a mistake, but what the hell? It was the first record I did in my life, and I didn't know I could say, "Hey, can I try it again?" I didn't know anything. I didn't even really know how to overdub. There are no overdubs except for very minimal stuff like on "Runnin' with the Devil" and "Jamie's Cryin'." The rest is just guitar panned hard left and blowin' live.

What do you remember about "Ain't Talkin' 'Bout Love"?
Believe it or not, it started as a punk rock parody. I just started slamming on two chords—A minor and G—and we were having a gas! Then I said, "Wait a minute, we can really make something out of this." We actually wrote three songs in Dave's basement that day. I remember one of them was called "Bullethead"—"B-b-b-b-b-b-b-bullethead." [*laughs*] It was actually a pretty good song.

It's funny you should mention that you were taking a shot at

ROSS HALFIN

punk. In the recently published book *Waiting for the Sun: The Sound of Los Angeles*, Van Halen is described as "...a hard rock/ metal quartet from Pasadena who at the eleventh hour had decided against becoming a punk band." The author obviously missed the point of what you were doing.

Yeah, and so did a lot of other people. You should see the first album cover Warner Bros. designed for us—they tried to make us look like the Clash. We said "Fuck this shit!" and came up with the Van Halen logo and made them put it on the album so that it would be clear that we had nothing to do with the punk movement.

It was our way of saying, "Hey, we're just a fucking rock and roll band, don't try and slot us with the Sex Pistols thing just because it's becoming popular."

What can you tell us about "Dance the Night Away"?

It ended up completely different from how I'd imagined it. When you're writing a piece of music and other people get involved, it always turns into something else. It ended up having an almost Latin flavor to it, which I don't really dig. Still, it's a nice song—a pop tune.

What about "And the Cradle Will Rock..."?

Oh man, that was hilarious. I spent two weeks of rehearsals just pounding out this groove on an old Wurlitzer electric piano through an MXR flanger and a stack of Marshalls. Al and I were having a cool time playing it, but the thing is I didn't have a clue where to take it. So we just kept hammering away every day for, I swear, two weeks. Finally, one chord came and it all snapped into shape. All the changes, the verse, the solo, the breakdown, all the pieces came after going nowhere for ages.

Do songs often reveal themselves to you in that fashion?
Sometimes they come complete. Sometimes you have to work on 'em. Sometimes nothing comes. But one thing is for certain: you gotta keep working to enable it to come. You can't just sit around and wait for an idea to hit you, even though that tends to happen to me a lot more now that I don't drink. It's a wicked feeling when a complete piece of music comes to you. But it's not me, I'm just a vehicle—and I really believe that.

I was chosen to do this, and the more sober I am, the clearer I am. I've been writing a lot lately. In fact, it's hard to stop—I just go and go and go. I even have a studio in the bathroom now. I have a Peavey Combo amp in there, two self-powered Genelec speakers, an Alesis 8-track digital recorder, a Linn drum machine, an AMS stereo digital delay, a DAT, a harmonizer, a cassette machine and a Mackie mixer. And a saxophone and a fretless bass. It's just a little too small to fit a keyboard in there. [*laughs*]

So it's been easier to compose since you gave up drinking?
Yeah, but it wasn't easy to convince myself that it would be. I swore to this therapist that there was no way that she would ever get me to write without a few beers. Drinking was the one thing I could count on to help me break down my inhibitions and loosen up. She said, "Give me 12 hours." I said, "You're wasting your time, it ain't gonna work." Then she had me do some yoga and some meditation and some chanting. And then we went outside and did a bunch of weird exercises for a half-hour, to the point where I almost passed out. And then she had me sit down and relax. Next she told me to close my eyes and "imagine the room that you go to after you've had a six-pack of beer. Really try and feel that place."

I sat there for a couple of minutes and said, "Yeah, I'm kinda there." I kept my eyes closed, she handed me a guitar and I just started writing. I couldn't believe it. It took only an hour! I ended up writing five songs that day, including the music for "Me Wise Magic." It blew my mind. I just didn't want to believe I could do it without drinking.

The therapist said, "Look, you've been chosen to do this, all you're doing by drinking is blocking it. It's a lot easier for them to send it when you're clear." I just refused to believe it, but she proved me wrong. And now I can't stop writing in what I now call my "room." My wife, Valerie, recently said, "The next time you see your therapist, ask her how to get out of that 'room' and into the bedroom!" [*laughs*]

Getting back to the songs: what about "Unchained"?
Ummm, what was I thinking? I don't have a clue. That whole album, *Fair Warning*, was kind of a dark period. I don't know whether it was fueled by anger or whatever, but I ended up doing 90 percent of the guitar stuff at four o'clock in the morning with our engineer, Donn Landee. Nothing was really being done during the day, so I'd go back down at night and do it.

"Jump"?
That was the first song I wrote that was recorded in my home studio, 5150.

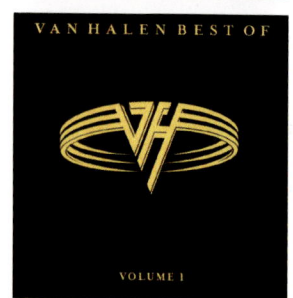

It was also a very important song for the band.
Yeah, and it's a pretty well-known fact that certain people didn't want me playing keyboards because they thought I should only be a "guitar hero."

"Panama"?
It was kind of AC/DC-inspired. We had just done a tour with them the year before. It was us, Mötley Crüe and AC/DC in 1983, in Europe, and just the power of those guys blew my mind—the constant "boom, boom, boom." They play the same song over and over, but it's a great song. They were probably one of the most powerful live bands I've ever seen in my life. The energy...they were just unstoppable.

I'll never forget our first big tour. It was a theater-sized tour—3,000 seaters. We headlined a bill featuring Ronnie Montrose and Journey. We were supposed to do 60 shows, but we left early because we had an offer to do "Day on the Green" [*a 1995 festival held in Oakland, California*]. I think Aerosmith and Foreigner were co-headlining.

We had our own trailer, and next door to us was AC/DC, who were also playing that day. Anyway, they went on before us, and I was standing on the side of the stage thinking, We have to follow these guys? They were so fuckin' powerful, but I remember feeling that we held our own. I was really happy. It blew my mind—I didn't think anybody could follow them.

"Why Can't This Be Love?" was your first big hit with Sammy Hagar. How did that come together?
I wrote that on an Oberheim OB-8 keyboard in my bedroom. It was one of the first songs where Sammy said, "You don't mind if I follow your keyboard melody, do you?" And I said, "No, not at all," though, in general, I don't really like the vocals to follow my instrumental lines. I'd much rather have the vocal line act as counterpoint. That's why I dig Glen Ballard, who produced the two new tracks on our *Best of Volume 1* album. He's always searching for great counter lines. Our conceptual goal was to put lyrics and a melody over [*sings the first four notes of Beethoven's Symphony No. 5*]. You know what I mean? What would you sing over that? But that would be the shit if it could be done. And that to me is the essence of a great and complete song: great music that stands on its own, great melodic music, great counter-vocal melody and great lyrics. And of course a good performance.

Do you believe you've reached those goals on any specific track?
I don't think you ever reach complete happiness. If you do, it's done, it's over with. What I thought was the shit two years ago just doesn't have the same impact on me now. I think it's just human nature to change, to get tired of the same thing...I don't know what it is. I'm always experimenting and dicking around, but not because of any goal. Music is my life, and it's very, very hard work, which a lot of other people don't understand. It's not a nine-to-five job—it's a 25-hour-a-day job.

"Dreams"?
That's the one song Mick Jones of Foreigner helped us produce. Mick was supposed to produce the whole *5150* album because Warner Bros. didn't trust us to do it on our own. But Foreigner were on the road while we were recording, so Mick really wasn't around much. So we would say, "Yeah, Mick's here producing." In the

meantime, I produced Sammy's vocal and Donn and I engineered. Mick got the credit, but *5150* was really a band-produced effort.

"Poundcake"?

Sometimes Al has a better ear for my playing than I do. I'll just play a hint of something, and he'll stop me and say, "That part right there." And more often than not, it will be something that will eventually evolve into a song. "Poundcake" came from Al recognizing the potential of a chord progression that I probably would have skipped over.

"Right Now" was another important milestone for the band.

It took 13 years to make that record. I wrote that song a long time ago—right around the "Jump" period. Some people thought "Right Now" was really risky, but to me, it's not even stepping out. It's still a rock tune. It's just piano-based, so what the fuck? It's not a headbanger. It's not like "Poundcake" or "Judgment Day," but it's still Van Halen.

If "Right Now" was considered risky, "Can't Stop Loving You" was one of your more overtly commercial songs.

Our producer at that time, Bruce Fairbairn, asked me if I had any pop ditties lying around. I had a ton of tapes, so at first I was just going to go through them to see if had anything. But I was just too lazy to dig through them all. Instead, I just decided it would be easier to write a

ion, if you compare them, the Wolfgang is a better guitar. It has a detuner on it, and the neck is angled back a bit so it's more comfortable to play. When I pick up a Music Man now it almost feels like it's bowed in. It's like playing a Les Paul and then picking up a Tele. It's a whole different feel. The neck has the same feel but the balance of the guitar is better, and I think it's better looking with the arch top. We're coming out with a tobacco sunburst, purple red, yellow, black and ivory. Six colors.

As far as the amp goes, I think the 5150 is a pretty respectable amp and, believe it or not, it's the only amp I've never blown up. You can unplug the speaker cord and keep playing and it won't blow. If you do that with a Marshall or Hi-Watt or anything else, it will just pop.

You've always described your ideal guitar tone as sounding "brown." Is that still true today?

That ball has been thrown around so much that it's hard to keep track of what it originally meant. It was actually Alex's term for the sound of his snare—the meaty sound of beating on a log. It also seemed like a good way to describe my ideal sound at the time. If you listen to *Van Halen*, though, my sound is actually pretty bright—it's not really "brown" at all. It cuts.

My guitar sound is fatter these days than it is on the old records. I feel kind of guilty sometimes, because I'm definitely hogging the spectrum of sound on our records. I'm using five amps and cabinets at the same time, all with two mikes on them. There's this guy in Vancouver

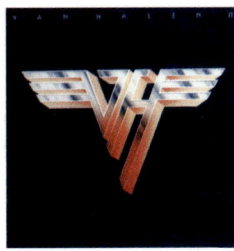 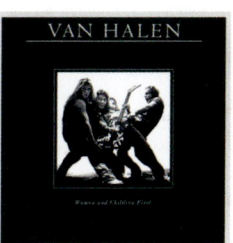   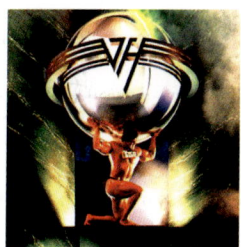

new tune from scratch—and "Can't Stop Loving You" was the result. I played it for him and he said, "Great." I think it was one of the last things we recorded for *Balance*.

What can you tell us about the new tracks with David Lee Roth? How did you compose "Me Wise Magic"?

That was just one of almost 20 songs I'd written in the previous couple of months. I played it for Dave, and at first he didn't quite care for it. Alex and I had already written a verse melody, and Dave wanted to do something where he sang more. But after playing 15 other pieces of music for him, we still couldn't find anything that inspired him.

After thinking about it, he decided to go back to "Me Wise Magic." And I went, "Okay, cool." At the time he thought it sounded angry, but I convinced him that the verse melody didn't sound angry, it just sounded like some kind of strange creature. And the chorus was undeniably majestic and powerful.

That song has major imagery for me. There are so many vibes to it; the verse is one thing, the chorus is another, the breakdown before the solo, the solo, and the whole fadeout. It's a ride!

Speaking of new songs, you recently switched to Peavey after playing Music Man guitars for several years. Why the change? And can you talk a little bit about the Wolfgang guitar?

Music Man and I had a falling out. I hope there are no hard feelings. The logical place to go was Peavey because they make my amps. And I really like working with them, it's a very family-oriented place. The Wolfgang is just a natural evolution from the Music Man, 75 percent of which I designed. I just never thought that the guitar was finished. I always wanted a cross between three guitars—a Les Paul, a Telecaster and a Strat—and the Wolfgang is the realization of that dream.

To me, it's just an updated version of the Music Man. And in my opin-

that made me this splitter box that allows me to use six amps simultaneously. I use three 5150s for dirt and two 5150s for clean, and each amp is on a different track. Also, each amp has two mikes on each cabinet, so you can change the sound of each.

So you're not using Marshalls at all any more?

I use them and Hi-Watts now and then. But the meat of the sound—the beef—are the 5150s.

What about the gear you use on the two new tracks? I think "Can't Get This Stuff No More" represents the first time you ever used a talk box.

Actually, Matt [*Bruck, Van Halen's guitar tech*] ran the talk box for me. My mouth wasn't big enough. I said to Glen, "You try it," because when I did it just sounded like a wah-wah. I didn't know you had to deep throat the damn thing! [*laughs*] Glen tried it first and said, "Fuck, it sounds the same as when you do it." Finally, Matt, who used one in his own band, tried it, and it sounded good.

Did you use one of those DigiTech Whammy Pedals on the solo to "Me Wise Magic"?

No, that's just the prototype Peavey with the Steinberger tremolo. And during the end I'm using a Fernandes sustainer.

What goes through your mind when you look back at all of this music?

I think it's been a hell of a ride. I think it shows growth and that we're always trying to get better at what we do. Each song is like a photograph—that's why we didn't re-mix anything. All we did was digitally remaster it so the sound quality would be better. Whatever magic was captured on each song, we wanted to leave intact. ▱

EDITORIAL
EDITOR-IN-CHIEF **Brad Tolinski**
MANAGING EDITOR **Jeff Kitts**
EXECUTIVE EDITOR **Christopher Scapelliti**
SENIOR EDITOR **Brad Angle**

ART
DESIGN DIRECTOR **Alexis Cook**
PHOTOGRAPHY DIRECTOR **Jimmy Hubbard**
DIGITAL IMAGING SPECIALIST **Evan Trusewicz**

PRODUCTION
PRODUCTION COORDINATOR **Nicole Schilling**

CONSUMER MARKETING
CONSUMER MARKETING DIRECTOR **Crystal Hudson**
AUDIENCE DEVELOPMENT COORDINATOR **Kara Tzinivis**
FULFILLMENT COORDINATOR **Ulises Cabrera**
MARKETING COORDINATOR **Dominique Rennell**

NEWBAY MEDIA CORPORATE
PRESIDENT & CEO **Steve Palm**
CHIEF FINANCIAL OFFICER **Paul Mastronardi**
CONTROLLER **Jack Liedke**
VICE PRESIDENT-PUBLISHING DIRECTOR, MUSIC GROUP **Bill Amstutz**
VICE PRESIDENT OF DIGITAL MEDIA **Joe Ferrick**
VICE PRESIDENT OF AUDIENCE DEVELOPMENT **Denise Robbins**
VICE PRESIDENT OF CONTENT & MARKETING **Anthony Savona**
VICE PRESIDENT OF HUMAN RESOURCES **Ray Vollmer**

TIME HOME ENTERTAINMENT
PUBLISHER **Jim Childs**
VICE PRESIDENT, BUSINESS DEVELOPMENT & STRATEGY **Steven Sandonato**
EXECUTIVE DIRECTOR, MARKETING SERVICES **Carol Pittard**
EXECUTIVE DIRECTOR, RETAIL & SPECIAL SALES **Tom Mifsud**
EXECUTIVE PUBLISHING DIRECTOR **Joy Butts**
EDITORIAL DIRECTOR **Stephen Koepp**
EDITORIAL OPERATIONS DIRECTOR **Michael Q. Bullerdick**
DIRECTOR, BOOKAZINE DEVELOPMENT & MARKETING **Laura Adam**
FINANCE DIRECTOR **Glenn Buonocore**
ASSOCIATE PUBLISHING DIRECTOR **Megan Pearlman**
ASSISTANT GENERAL COUNSEL **Helen Wan**
ASSISTANT DIRECTOR, SPECIAL SALES **Ilene Schreider**
SENIOR BOOK PRODUCTION MANAGER **Susan Chodakiewicz**
DESIGN & PREPRESS MANAGER **Anne-Michelle Gallero**
BRAND MANAGER **Katie McHugh**
ASSOCIATE PREPRESS MANAGER **Alex Voznesenskiy**

SPECIAL THANKS
Christine Austin, Jeremy Biloon, Rose Cirrincione, Lauren Hall Clark, Jacqueline Fitzgerald,
Christine Font, Jenna Goldberg, Hillary Hirsch, Suzanne Janso, David Kahn,
Mona Li, Amy Mangus, Robert Marasco, Kimberly Marshall, Amy Migliaccio,
Nina Mistry, Dave Rozzelle, Adriana Tierno, Vanessa Wu

SUBSCRIBER CUSTOMER SERVICE: **Guitar World Magazine Customer Care**, P.O. Box 6305, Harlan, IA 51593-1805
ONLINE: **www.guitarworld.com/customerservice** PHONE: **1-800-456-6441** EMAIL: **GWOcustserv@cdsfulfillment.com**

BACK ISSUES: **Please visit our store: www.guitarworld.com/store**

EDITORIAL AND ADVERTISING OFFICES
28 East 28th Street, 9th Floor, New York, NY 10016 (212) 768-2966; FAX: (212) 944-9279

NEWBAY MEDIA, LLC
28 East 28th Street, 12th Floor, New York, NY 10016 www.nbmedia.com